W9-AFE-858

CONTEMPORARY'S
GED
TEST 2: SOCIAL STUDIES
EXERCISE BOOK

CB
CONTEMPORARY BOOKS

a division of NTC/CONTEMPORARY PUBLISHING GROUP
Lincolnwood, Illinois USA

Writer: Karen Scott Digilio

ISBN: 0-8092-4541-8

Published by Contemporary Books,
a division of NTC/Contemporary Publishing Group, Inc.,
4255 West Touhy Avenue,
Lincolnwood (Chicago), Illinois 60646-1975 U.S.A.

Contents

Acknowledgments

Excerpt on page 1 from *A Pictorial History of the Civil War Years* by Paul M. Angle. Copyright © 1967 by Nelson Doubleday, Inc. Reprinted with permission of Doubleday, a division of Bantam, Doubleday, Dell Publishing Group, Inc.

Excerpt on page 2 from *Bury My Heart at Wounded Knee* by Dee Brown. Copyright © 1971 by Henry Holt and Company, Inc. Reprinted with permission.

Excerpt on page 2 from *The Making of the President 1960* by Theodore W. White. Copyright © 1961. Atheneum House, Inc. Reprinted with permission of Macmillan Publishing Company.

Excerpt on page 5 from *America the Melting Pot* by Patricia Pomboy Mintz. Copyright © 1969 Charles Scribner's Sons.

Excerpt on page 8 from *The Right Stuff* by Tom Wolfe. Copyright © 1979 by Tom Wolfe. Reprinted by permission of Farrar, Straus and Giroux, Inc.

Excerpt on page 9 from "Remembering the Crash of '29" by Tom Tiede. Copyright © 1987 Tom Tiede and Newspaper Enterprise Association. Reprinted with permission.

Cartoon on page 10 by Roy Osrin courtesy of the *Cleveland Plain Dealer*.

Excerpt on page 13 from *The Jungle* by Upton Sinclair.

Cartoon on page 15 by Charles Pearson. Copyright © Charles Pearson/Rothco. Reprinted by permission.

Excerpt on page 26 from *Alone in a Crowd: Women in the Trades Tell Their Stories* by Jean Reith Schroedel. Copyright © 1985 by Temple University. Reprinted with permission.

Cartoon on page 26 by Glen Dines. Reprinted with permission.

Excerpt on page 27 from *The Blue Capricorn* by Eugene Burdick. Copyright © 1961 by Eugene Burdick. Reprinted by permission of Houghton Mifflin Company.

Excerpt on page 27 from *Bus 9 to Paradise* by Leo F. Buscaglia, Ph.D. Reprinted with permission.

Excerpt on page 30 from *Mothers Who Work: Strategies for Coping* by Jeanne Brodin and Bonnie Mitelman, copyright © 1983 by Ballantine Books, a division of Random House, Inc. Reprinted with permission.

Graph on page 31 from *Anthropology* by E. Adamson Hoebel. Copyright © 1966 by McGraw-Hill Book Company. Reprinted by permission.

Chart on page 33 from *The Ethnic Almanac* by Stephanie Bernardo. Copyright © 1981 by Stephanie Bernardo. Reprinted by permission of Doubleday, a division of Bantam, Doubleday, Dell Publishing Group, Inc.

Map on page 36 adapted from *The First Book Atlas*, edited by Hammond Incorporated. Reprinted with permission of the publisher, Franklin Watts.

Table on page 49 from "A Campaign to Balance the Budget" by Bill Powell, Eleanor Clift, Rich Thomas, Tim Noah, and Sylvester Monroe. Copyright © 1987 by *Newsweek*. Reprinted by permission.

Excerpt on page 50 from "Put Issues on Ice Until January '88" by William Neikirk. Copyright © 1987, Chicago Tribune Company, all rights reserved, used with permission.

Cartoon on page 52 by S. Kelly. Copyright © 1987. Reprinted with permission of the Copley News Service.

Table on page 57 from *The Entrepreneurs: Explorations Within the American Business Tradition* by Robert Sobel. Copyright © 1974.

Cartoon on page 59 by Mike Keefe, de Pixion Features © 1994. Reprinted by permission.

Cartoon on page 61 by Jeff Danziger in *The Christian Science Monitor*. Copyright © 1987 TCSPS. Reprinted by permission.

Cartoon on page 62 by Mike Keefe, de Pixion Features © 1994. Reprinted by permission.

Chart on page 70 from Time Inc. Copyright © 1988. Reprinted by permission from TIME.

The editor has made every effort to trace the ownership of all copyrighted material, and necessary permissions have been secured in most cases. Should there prove to be any question regarding the use of any material, regret is hereby expressed for such error. Upon notification of any such oversight, proper acknowledgment will be made in future editions.

Introduction

Welcome to *Contemporary's GED Social Studies Exercise Book*. The purpose of this book is to provide you with additional practice in answering the types of questions that will appear on the actual GED Social Studies Test. The organization of this exercise book parallels that of *GED Test 2: Social Studies*, the satellite book, so if you need more in-depth review or further instruction, refer to this book.

This exercise book is divided into the five content areas of social studies that will be covered on the test. These content areas and their respective percentages of the entire test are:

Content Area	Percentage of Test
U.S. History	25%
Political Science	20%
Behavioral Sciences	20%
Economics	20%
Geography	15%

Reading Skills

The GED Social Studies Test also will require that you use certain reasoning and thinking skills in answering the questions. The thinking skills and their percentages of the test are:

Skill	Percentage of Test
Comprehension	20%
Application	30%
Analysis	30%
Evaluation	20%

In addition to the reading passages found throughout this exercise book, you will find many visuals such as charts, maps, graphs, and editorial cartoons. These kinds of visuals make up about 30 percent of the actual test.

A complete answer key that explains the correct answer tells you why a certain answer is the correct choice. This helps you to improve your skill in answering multiple-choice questions.

Practice Test

We recommend that you take the practice test at the end of this book to determine whether you are ready to take the real GED Social Studies Test. The test includes 60 multiple-choice questions—approximately the same number as the real test contains. Since you will be given 85 minutes to complete the real test, we recommend that you time yourself accordingly when taking the practice test in this book.

Evaluation Chart

Finally, to help you pinpoint those areas in which you may need additional practice, an evaluation chart is provided on page 75. This chart identifies each question on the practice test according to the content area and reading skill. For additional practice you can refer to *GED Test 2: Social Studies*, which devotes a separate chapter to each skill.

At the beginning of each section in this exercise book, you'll see references to *text pages*. These page numbers refer to *Contemporary's GED Test 2: Social Studies*. Go back to the appropriate pages whenever you need a review.

U.S. History

Text pages
91–143

Questions 1 and 2 are based on the following passage.

October comes to South Carolina as a blessed interlude between hot summer and chill and rainy winter. In the tenth month of the year the skies are blue, the breezes warm, the flowers still verdant.[1] But in October, 1860, the amenity[2] of nature did not soften the hard resolution of William Henry Gist, governor of the state. For years this fifty-three-year-old man who had divided his life between politics, his plantation, and the Methodist church had been determined that the South should set itself up as an independent nation.

———————
[1] *verdant*—green
[2] *amenity*—agreeableness

1. South Carolina was the first state to secede from the Union in 1860. This passage implies that Governor Gist

   (1) was opposed to secession, but was overruled
   (2) tried to remain neutral as long as he could
   (3) was convinced by other politicians to support secession
   (4) became aware of the idea of secession late in life
   (5) was an instigator of the idea of secession

2. According to this passage, Governor Gist valued most highly

   (1) homeland and religion
   (2) the beauty of South Carolina
   (3) the power of the federal government
   (4) determination and humanity
   (5) the personal rights of individuals

Questions 3 and 4 are based on the following passage.

Though the United States and most of Europe experienced an industrial revolution during the latter half of the nineteenth century, the tremendous change from manual production to mechanical did not affect much of the Third World until recent years. As a result, many of the problems associated with industrialization have not affected these countries until recently. Now countries like South Korea are finding its workers objecting violently to long hours and low pay. The end result is that while the influence of labor organizations is at a low point in Japan and the United States, unions are increasing in power in South Korea. The power of labor organizations has increased to such an extent that they can stop the flow of work and, therefore, the flow of capital in a still struggling economy.

3. The author of the above passage makes the judgment that Third World labor unions could

   (1) cripple the developing economies of their own countries
   (2) damage the economies of other industrialized countries
   (3) raise wages unreasonably high for laborers in their own countries
   (4) lengthen working hours for laborers in their own countries
   (5) worsen the working conditions for laborers in all countries

4. The author makes the unstated assumption that

   (1) industrialization causes low wages and long hours
   (2) industrialization increases wages for laborers in manufacturing
   (3) industrialization did not come to Third World countries until recently
   (4) in South Korea, labor unions are beneficial to workers and not to a nation's economy
   (5) industrialization does not necessarily mean mechanization

ANSWERS ARE ON PAGE 76.

Questions 5–9 are based on the following passage.

The ring of axes and the crash of falling trees echoed up and down the coasts of the land which the white man now called New England. Settlements began crowding in upon each other. In 1625 some of the colonists asked Samoset to give them twelve thousand additional acres of Pemaquid land. Samoset knew that land came from the Great Spirit, was as endless as the sky, and belonged to no man. To humor these strangers in their strange ways, however, he went through a ceremony of transferring the land and made his mark on a paper for them. It was the first deed of Indian land to English colonists.

5. Samoset was

   (1) a British colonist
   (2) an American builder
   (3) a European trader
   (4) an Indian leader
   (5) a religious fanatic

6. The Dutch's purchase of Manhattan Island from local Indians for $24 worth of kettles and beads supports the conclusion that Samoset and other Indians

   (1) did not know and appreciate the true value of land
   (2) were tricked into selling their land for so little
   (3) did not conceive of property ownership in the same way as Europeans did
   (4) prized shiny trinkets and utensils more than they prized land
   (5) are very bighearted people when it comes to giving

7. The purchase of Manhattan Island by the Dutch and Samoset's deeding of the Pemaquid land to white settlers for a nominal sum demonstrate the American belief that money

   (1) is the root of all evil
   (2) can buy anything
   (3) cannot buy happiness
   (4) does not grow on trees
   (5) makes money

8. Which of the following statements contains a faulty conclusion?

   (1) If land belongs to no man, then no one can deed it.
   (2) If the Great Spirit provides land, then it is as endless as the sky.
   (3) If land belongs to no man, then it cannot belong to Indians.
   (4) If the Great Spirit provides land, then it really belongs to Him alone.
   (5) If land had to be deeded to the Europeans, then they must have believed the Indians really owned it.

9. The "Great Spirit" is another name for

   (1) the chief of the Pemaquid tribe
   (2) the king of England
   (3) a Supreme Being
   (4) Mother Nature
   (5) Father Time

Questions 10 and 11 are based on the following quote.

"Mister," said a Chicago Negro discussing his vote with me in 1960, "they could put a dog at the head of that ticket and if they called him Democratic I'd vote for him. This hoolarium about civil rights doesn't mean anything to me—it's the man who puts money into my pocket that counts."

10. From this quote you can infer the voter feels that

   (1) civil rights activists have not helped the cause of minorities
   (2) civil rights activists pressure politicians for jobs for minorities
   (3) Democratic presidents improve economic conditions for minorities more than Republican presidents do
   (4) Democratic presidents do not improve the economic conditions for minorities
   (5) Democratic and Republican politicians are equally insensitive to the needs of minorities

11. The man being quoted places a high value on

   (1) financial security
   (2) political loyalty
   (3) racial equality
   (4) civil liberties
   (5) moral standards

ANSWERS ARE ON PAGE 76.

Questions 12 and 13 are based on the following map.

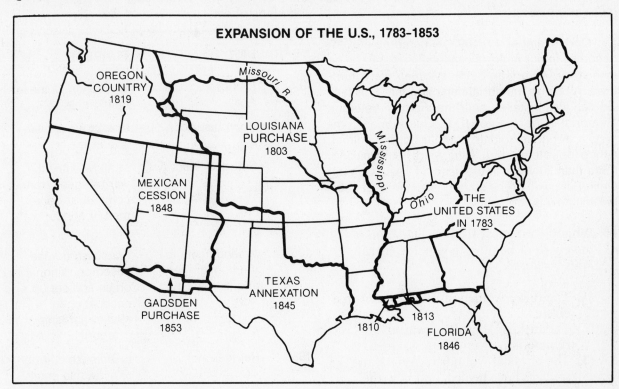

EXPANSION OF THE U.S., 1783–1853

12. Which of the following states was *not* part of the United States in 1783?

    (1) New York
    (2) Virginia
    (3) Florida
    (4) Georgia
    (5) South Carolina

13. California was brought within the borders of the United States under the

    (1) Oregon Country Settlement
    (2) Mexican Cession
    (3) Gadsden Purchase
    (4) Texas Annexation
    (5) Louisiana Purchase

14. Which of the following national moods resulted most directly from the Louisiana Purchase?

    (1) a demand that foreign powers not interfere in the Americas
    (2) an intense desire for further territorial expansion
    (3) strong loyalty to one's native region above all others
    (4) the belief that Americans must care for the less fortunate countries
    (5) a belief in the need to maintain good relations with other nations

ANSWERS ARE ON PAGE 76.

Questions 15 and 16 are based on the following passage.

On November 11, 1993, a memorable event occurred in our nation's capital. For the first time in history, American servicewomen were honored. A bronze memorial depicting three military women was installed near the Vietnam Veterans Memorial in Washington, D.C. One woman comforts a wounded soldier, another holds a helmet, a third looks to the sky. "Nine years in the making, more than 20 years in the needing," said General Colin L. Powell of the statue. "The circle of healing will now be complete."

15. Which is the most likely explanation of the circle of healing to which General Powell refers?

   (1) The three women in the statue sit in a circle.
   (2) The historical cycle of war and rebirth is now ended.
   (3) The physical wounds of American soldiers have healed, and now the statue heals their wounded spirits.
   (4) Female nurses healed America's soldiers during the war, and now, through the statue, America helps heal their psychological wounds.
   (5) The United States has repaired diplomatic relations with Vietnam, and now it has repaired damage done by the war at home.

16. What is the most likely reason the statue does not show women fighting?

   (1) American women did not participate in combat during the Vietnam War.
   (2) The U.S. government has still not officially admitted that U.S. soldiers fought in Vietnam.
   (3) Families visiting the statue might be offended by the violence depicted.
   (4) Vietnam Vets would consider this a negative image of American soldiers.
   (5) The sculptor did not want to traumatize Vietnam Vets by reminding them of wartime violence.

Questions 17 and 18 are based on the following chart.

YEAR	LAW	PURPOSE
1882	Chinese Exclusion Act	to exclude Chinese immigrants
1917	Anarchist Act	to exclude subversive aliens
1953	Refugee Relief Act	to allow entry for war refugees from communist countries or Middle East
1965	Amendments to the Immigration and Nationality Acts	to abolish quotas based on national origin and set up occupation-related hardship categories
1980	Refugee Act	to increase number of allowable immigrants and redefine word "refugee"

17. In general, the purpose of the United States immigration laws over the years has been to

   (1) exclude certain races from entering the United States
   (2) allow the largest numbers of immigrants possible into the United States
   (3) increase restrictions on the number of immigrants to the United States
   (4) control the types of people who could immigrate into the United States
   (5) eliminate the need for quotas in future immigration laws

18. Which of the following laws gave special consideration to immigrants who were members of underrepresented professions in the United States?

   (1) The 1882 Chinese Exclusion Act
   (2) The 1917 Anarchist Act
   (3) The 1953 Refugee Relief Act
   (4) The 1965 amendments to the Immigration and Nationality Acts
   (5) The 1980 Refugee Act

ANSWERS ARE ON PAGES 76-77.

Questions 19–21 are based on the following passage.

Addressing four thousand naturalized citizens at Philadelphia in May 1915, Woodrow Wilson, the twenty-seventh president of the United States, expressed his belief that the immigrant served the unique purpose of constantly reminding the American citizen that this was a nation dedicated to the principle of equality of opportunity and justice for all. Just three days before this speech was given, the Lusitania had been sunk by the Germans with the loss of 1,198 lives. It was expected that Wilson in this, his first major speech after the tragedy, would call for immediate retaliation. Instead, he spoke of America as the example of peace, for "peace is the healing and elevating influence of the world and strife is not." He suggested that a great nation must be "too proud to fight." It was only after a time that most people realized that his arguments held a significance far surpassing easy thought of revenge.

19. According to this passage, which of the following can we infer to have been most highly valued by Woodrow Wilson?

(1) equality of opportunity
(2) justice for all people
(3) pride in our country
(4) peace in the world
(5) revenge at any cost

20. What opinion about Woodrow Wilson is suggested by this passage?

(1) Wilson spoke of America as an example of peace.
(2) Wilson was an eloquent and forceful speaker.
(3) Wilson believed America to be a nation of opportunity and justice.
(4) Wilson should have retaliated against the Germans immediately.
(5) Wilson was wise not to seek quick revenge against the Germans.

21. Which is a more recent example of a president of the United States choosing peace over strife?

(1) Bush's liberation of Kuwait in the Gulf War
(2) Kennedy's ordering of a blockade of Cuba to keep Russians out
(3) Johnson's escalation of the war in Vietnam to save face for the United States
(4) Carter's refusal to send troops immediately to rescue American hostages in Iran
(5) Ford's pardoning Nixon of any responsibility as a result of Watergate

Questions 22 and 23 are based on the following passage.

On October 19, 1781, the British surrendered to the Americans at the Battle of Yorktown after six-and-a-half years of long winters, hand-to-hand battles, and the loss of many lives. The Revolutionary War is an example of a victory won by the side with the fewest resources and soldiers, the scarcest amount of food, and the least money. The American Army defeated the greatest superpower at that time by an abundance of spirit for the cause, strong leadership, and generous contributions of help and support from the French. Ultimately, too, Britain's lack of belief in their own cause contributed to their own defeat.

22. The colonists' position in the Revolutionary War was most similar to which of the following?

(1) The resource-rich Americans during World War II
(2) The powerful Russians in the war in Afghanistan
(3) The American-supported South Koreans during the Korean conflict
(4) The poor but idealistic Vietcong during the Vietnam War
(5) The government-controlled Chinese army during their Cultural Revolution

ANSWERS ARE ON PAGE 77.

23. According to this writer, which country had the most powerful military in 1781?

    (1) the United States
    (2) France
    (3) Russia
    (4) Great Britain
    (5) Canada

Questions 24 and 25 are based on the following terms:

Niagara Movement—a movement to fully end discrimination and segregation in the United States

American Missionary Association—a movement of Christian teachers who went South after the Civil War to volunteer their teaching services

United Negro Improvement Association—a separatist movement of black Americans who launched a "back to Africa" movement

the Underground Railroad—a movement organized before the Civil War to help slaves escape to Canada

populist movement—a political movement in which black and white farmers united to try to overcome oppressive conditions

24. Which of the following was a forerunner of the moderate, urban National Association for the Advancement of Colored People (NAACP)?

    (1) Niagara Movement
    (2) American Missionary Association
    (3) United Negro Improvement Association
    (4) The Underground Railroad
    (5) Populist Movement

25. Which of the following would have been described as the "early American Peace Corps"?

    (1) Niagara Movement
    (2) American Missionary Association
    (3) United Negro Improvement Association
    (4) The Underground Railroad
    (5) Populist Movement

Questions 26 and 27 are based on the following passage.

The German Jews who fled from Hitler were different from the ghetto and eastern European Jews. They were not devout Zionists but had largely been assimilated into German society. They were not pioneers and merchants; they were doctors and lawyers and scientists and artisans.

26. This passage implies that the ghetto and eastern European Jews were not usually

    (1) devoutly religious
    (2) professional workers
    (3) adventurous pioneers
    (4) ambitious merchants
    (5) urban residents

27. The writer of this passage assumes that

    (1) devout Zionists do not easily assimilate into cultures around them
    (2) German Jews are less ambitious than their other European counterparts
    (3) European Jews are seldom able to handle full-time jobs
    (4) devout Zionists are easily assimilated into cultures around them
    (5) German Jews were different from other European Jews

28. In 1763 the British king proclaimed that no white settlers were to live west of the Appalachian mountains, leaving that territory temporarily to the Indians and French explorers and traders.

    Which statement is *not* a logical conclusion that follows from this fact?

    (1) Eventually, white settlers were able to cross the Proclamation Line of 1763.
    (2) French explorers and traders were not considered settlers since they did not stay long in any one place.
    (3) The British king still had much ruling power over the American colonies in 1763.
    (4) The Indians pressured the British king to make the Proclamation of 1763.
    (5) The Appalachian mountains were chosen as a boundary since they formed a natural barrier to westward movement.

ANSWERS ARE ON PAGE 77.

Questions 29 and 30 are based on the following map.

ESTIMATED SLAVE IMPORTS TO THE WEST—1400–1800

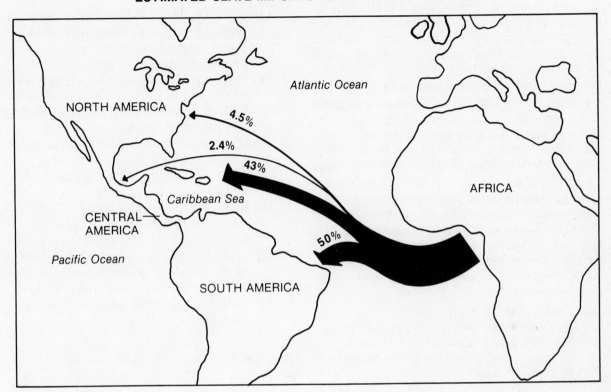

29. According to this map, which region imported the most slaves from the fifteenth to the nineteenth century?

  (1) Canada
  (2) The United States
  (3) Central America
  (4) The Caribbean
  (5) South America

30. Which of the following statements can be adequately supported by this map?

  (1) Generally, fifteenth-century slaves were better treated than nineteenth-century slaves.
  (2) Cultivation of sugar cane created the major demand for slaves in the Caribbean.
  (3) Slavery was not a new idea to mankind when it was introduced into the Americas.
  (4) Though the Caribbean region is smaller in territory than North and South America, proportionately it imported more slaves.
  (5) Canada did not import slaves because of moral objections.

ANSWERS ARE ON PAGE 77.

Questions 31–33 are based on the following passage.

The Soviet program gave off an aura of sorcery. The Soviets released practically no figures, pictures, or diagrams. And no names; it was revealed only that the Soviet program was guided by a mysterious individual known as "The Chief Designer." But his powers were indisputable! Every time the United States announced a great space experiment, the Chief Designer accomplished it first, in the most startling fashion. In 1955 the United States announces plans to launch an artificial earth satellite by early 1958. The Chief Designer startles the world by doing it in October 1957. The United States announces plans to send a satellite into orbit around the sun in March of 1959. The Chief Designer does it in January 1959. The fact that the United States went ahead and successfully conducted such experiments on schedule, as announced, impressed no one—and Americans least of all.

31. The Americans were not impressed by their own country's accomplishments in the space program of the 1950s because the United States

    (1) was always behind in the schedule it had set
    (2) always accomplished its goals after the Soviets had
    (3) engineers did not have the same resources as the Soviet Chief Designer
    (4) would not cooperate with the Soviet Chief Designer
    (5) engineers did not make their plans as well known as the Soviets did

32. Which of the following characteristics did the American public of the 1950s value most highly during the progress of the space programs?

    (1) patriotism
    (2) carefulness
    (3) swiftness
    (4) materialism
    (5) mysteriousness

33. Which one of the following is a logical conclusion, based on the information given in the passage?

    (1) If the Chief Designer had revealed his plans to the world, then the United States might have made faster progress in its space program.
    (2) If the Chief Designer had worked for the United States, then America might have accomplished its space program advancements earlier.
    (3) If the Chief Designer had not beat the United States' deadline, then the Americans might not have met them on time.
    (4) If the Chief Designer had worked for any country other than Russia, then he might not have been so successful.
    (5) If the United States had found a way to put someone on the moon in July 1959, the Soviets would most likely have accomplished the same feat by May 1959.

Question 34 is based on the following statement.

While the generals and the politicians were calling the shots in Managua and Washington, the Nicaraguan people were struggling to hang on to their lives, their property, and their homes.

34. Which of the following is an opinion expressed by this writer?

    (1) Politicians and generals were running the war in Nicaragua.
    (2) The U.S. government was supporting the wrong side in the Nicaraguan War.
    (3) The U.S. government was morally right in supporting the Nicaraguan rebels.
    (4) The common people of Nicaragua objected very strongly to the war there.
    (5) The common people of Nicaragua were the big losers in the war there.

ANSWERS ARE ON PAGE 77.

Questions 35–38 are based on the following passage.

Sipe was a young dairy farmer in Kansas at the time. He was land rich and apparently secure by the standards of the day, and then the stock market crashed in October 1929; he was wiped out by the worldwide depression that followed. . . .

Agnes Gellan of Fargo, N.D., says that two-thirds of the banks in that state closed during the turmoil, and a third of the population went on welfare. She says 90,000 people fled the state to seek relief in other places, and many of those who stayed adopted socialistic politics to survive.

Bruce Medaris of Athens, Georgia, was between military enlistments when the market failed. He says he had $100,000 in securities and no idea they were in any particular danger. He says he lost everything except $100, "and I spent that on a suit of clothes, so I could begin my new life in style."

And Dellie Norton of Canton, N.C. She was raised in Appalachia, where prosperity went instantly from little to none: "I remember one Christmas we gave each other an apple. A single apple. I gave it to my mother who took a bite, she gave it to my father who took a bite, and I got it back to finish. . . ."

Sipe wonders if people today would be as pliable under the circumstances. The others I've interviewed wonder as well. They think Americans of the 1930s were "a more formidable breed," as Sipe puts it. They were raised on adversities, and they had the psychological skills to cope with terrible change.

35. Which of the following is an opinion expressed by one of the survivors of the Great Depression?

   (1) "He was land-rich and apparently secure by the standards of the day."
   (2) "Many of those who stayed adopted socialistic politics to survive."
   (3) "I lost everything except $100, and I spent that on a suit of clothes."
   (4) "Prosperity went instantly from little to none."
   (5) "Americans of the 1930s were 'a more formidable breed.'"

36. The most direct cause of the worldwide depression described in this passage was the

   (1) adoption of socialistic politics by many Americans
   (2) closing of over half the banks in the United States
   (3) huge numbers of people seeking welfare relief
   (4) lack of a strong American military
   (5) stock market crash in the United States

37. It can be concluded that this passage was written by

   (1) a psychologist researching the effect of the Depression
   (2) an economist studying the causes of the Depression
   (3) someone who is very critical of today's Americans
   (4) one of the survivors of the 1929 Great Depression
   (5) someone who interviewed survivors of the Great Depression

38. A region of the United States that frequently suffers economic depression is

   (1) the Great Lakes states
   (2) the Pacific coast
   (3) the Southwest
   (4) the Corn Belt
   (5) Appalachia

ANSWERS ARE ON PAGES 77-78.

Questions 39–41 are based on the following cartoon.

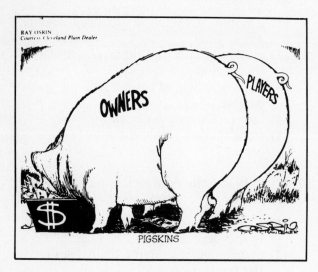

RAY OSRIN
Courtesy Cleveland Plain Dealer

OWNERS

PLAYERS

$

PIGSKINS

39. The cartoonist is expressing an opinion about

    (1) the hog market
    (2) farmers' problems
    (3) a football strike
    (4) drug use in sports
    (5) sports fans

40. The cartoonist's opinion about owners and players is that owners

    (1) are greedy; players are not
    (2) are not greedy, but players are
    (3) and players are greedy
    (4) take advantage of players
    (5) are not respected by players

41. Which of the following is a conclusion that can be supported by the cartoon?

    (1) If owners knew how negative their image was, they would give the players more money.
    (2) If players knew how negative their image was, they would not ask for so much money.
    (3) If owners and players did not accept bribes, they would not be so rich.
    (4) If owners and players could both earn more money, their salaries would be fair.
    (5) If players and owners want to solve their problems, they should both give in on money demands.

Questions 42 and 43 are based on the passage below.

    The English settled along the eastern coastline in North America and founded settlements in three distinct geographic regions. The founding purposes of the territories in each of these regions were religious freedom, fur trade, and farming.

    The New England colonies were founded primarily for religious freedom. These colonies included Massachusetts, New Hampshire, Rhode Island, and Connecticut. The middle colonies were founded primarily for fur trading and grain farming. These colonies included New York, New Jersey, Pennsylvania, Delaware, and Maryland. The southern colonies, which were favored by a warm climate, were founded for large-scale farming. These included Virginia, North Carolina, South Carolina, and Georgia.

42. The purpose of this passage is to

    (1) compare and contrast the thirteen colonies
    (2) describe the colonists' motives for settling in different regions
    (3) describe the geographical features of the land along the eastern seaboard
    (4) show why slavery could originate only in the southern colonies
    (5) divide the New World into specific territories

43. Which of the thirteen colonies described in the passage was founded for economic reasons as well as for religious reasons and is still associated with a prominent religious group?

    (1) Delaware
    (2) Rhode Island
    (3) South Carolina
    (4) Pennsylvania
    (5) Connecticut

ANSWERS ARE ON PAGE 78.

Questions 44–48 are based on the following passage.

There seems to be no end to media attacks on Bill Clinton because of alleged womanizing during the presidential campaign and his days as governor of Arkansas. These attacks are just another chapter in the media's intrusion into a politician's personal life for the entertainment value it offers. The public's fascination with presidents' private lives is no recent phenomenon, however, and the media have long recognized that this prurient interest sells papers and increases ratings.

President Andrew Jackson was accused in his day of engaging in adultery when he wed his previously married wife before her divorce was actually final, a fact of which he was not aware.

Grover Cleveland, who admitted to having fathered an illegitimate child before he ran for high office, was caricatured in the papers and taunted with the slogan "Ma, Ma, where's my Pa? Gone to the White House, ha, ha, ha!"

Warren Harding reputedly had an affair and fathered a child in a White House broom closet!

By and large, the American people want most of all to be entertained—not informed of the facts. One need only to consider the sales figures for magazines like *People Weekly* and scandal sheets like *The National Star* and *National Enquirer* to be aware of this fact.

44. The author of this passage

- **(1)** criticizes the media for intruding into politicians' lives
- **(2)** blames the public for supporting certain politicians
- **(3)** supports the presidency of Bill Clinton
- **(4)** rejects the presidency of Bill Clinton
- **(5)** believes that only "squeaky clean" candidates should be president

45. The author makes the assumption that

- **(1)** the behavior of politicians is of no interest to the American public
- **(2)** the media are not concerned about reporting the facts as they find them
- **(3)** the American public is willing to forgive politicians who make mistakes
- **(4)** the focus on the behavior of presidents is new
- **(5)** the media are the natural enemy of politicians

46. The writer is of the opinion that

- **(1)** American voters are uninformed
- **(2)** everyone has something to hide
- **(3)** the media are exercising their authority properly
- **(4)** wrongdoing by presidents will not be tolerated by the public
- **(5)** the media are giving the public precisely what it wants

47. Many people argue that mistakes made by a private citizen before he seeks office should not be held to the same standard of scrutiny as those made by a candidate or a politician in office. These people would say that this editorial unfairly compares

- **(1)** Clinton's behavior as governor with his behavior as a candidate
- **(2)** Clinton's behavior as governor with Cleveland's behavior as a private citizen
- **(3)** Clinton's behavior as a candidate with Cleveland's behavior as president
- **(4)** Cleveland's behavior as president with Harding's behavior as president
- **(5)** Jackson's behavior as president with Jackson's behavior as a candidate

48. Which of the following is *not* an idea supported by facts in this editorial?

- **(1)** People like to hear gossip about people in the public eye.
- **(2)** Mistakes made by presidents are not new.
- **(3)** The office of president of the United States demands the highest standards of conduct.
- **(4)** The media are just as guilty of engaging in sensationalism as the public is.
- **(5)** Scandal sells papers and increases ratings.

ANSWERS ARE ON PAGE 78.

Questions 49–52 are based on the following quote.

"With the existing colonies and dependencies of any European Power we have not interfered and shall not interfere. But with the governments who have declared their independence and maintained it, and whose independence we have, on great consideration and just principles acknowledged, we could not view any interposition for the purpose of oppressing them, or controlling in any other manner their destiny, by any European Power, in any other light than a manifestation of an unfriendly disposition towards the United States."

The Monroe Doctrine

49. Which of the following historical events did the U.S. government view as a display of "an unfriendly disposition toward the United States" as defined by the Monroe Doctrine?

(1) the victory of the Liberal Party in Canada in the 1940s
(2) the ousting of President Juan Peron by a military coup in Argentina in the 1950s
(3) the building up of missiles in Cuba by Russia in the 1960s
(4) the anti-American demonstrations in Puerto Rico in the 1970s
(5) the arrival of Cuban prisoners on United States shores in the 1980s

50. Which of the following foreign policy positions most closely describes the Monroe Doctrine?

(1) *imperialism*—the policy of one nation extending its authority over other territories or nations
(2) *isolationism*—the policy of noninterference in world affairs
(3) *nationalism*—the belief that the welfare of one's own nation must be put ahead of that of others
(4) *jingoism*—a policy of extreme nationalism characterized by frequent threats of warlike actions
(5) *internationalism*—the position that one nation's actions affects every other nation

51. Which of the following interpretations of the Monroe Doctrine by a U.S. president did Latin American governments view unfavorably?

(1) James Polk's warning against diplomatic and armed interference in the Americas by outside countries
(2) Grover Cleveland's use of the doctrine to help settle a boundary dispute between Venezuela and British Guiana
(3) Theodore Roosevelt's proclamation that the United States would intervene in the affairs of a Latin American government if it were threatened by European interference
(4) Franklin Roosevelt's "good neighbor policy" that gave expression to the idea that all American countries shared similar community interests
(5) John Kennedy's development of the Alliance for Progress that promised technical and financial cooperation among American nations

52. The year 1864 was not a good one for the United States. The Civil War was raging and, farther south, France was attempting to establish an empire in Mexico. The Secretary of State at the time, William Seward, diplomatically negotiated the withdrawal of the European trespasser and gained prestige for himself, the United States, and the Monroe Doctrine.

Which of the following statements is *not* a logical reason for Seward to have gained such prestige for his handling of the situation?

(1) War with France was avoided.
(2) Mexico was saved from domination by a foreign power.
(3) The American Civil War ended sooner.
(4) The strength of a policy declared years earlier was proven.
(5) A European country backed down from the still-young United States.

ANSWERS ARE ON PAGE 78.

Questions 53–55 are based on the following statement.

In a pastoral letter on the U.S. economy in 1986, several U.S. Catholic bishops wrote that "foreign investors, attracted by low wages in less developed countries, should consider both the potential loss of jobs in the home country and the potential exploitation of workers in the host country."

53. This statement would *best* apply to

(1) Third World labor unions striking for higher wages

(2) international corporations hiring cheap foreign labor

(3) American workers who protest the use of foreign labor

(4) missionaries in foreign countries who support workers there

(5) Third World governments that demand fair labor practices from foreign investors

54. In its statement, the committee of American Catholic bishops supported which value?

(1) private profit over nationalism

(2) nationalism over private profit

(3) economic fairness over private profit

(4) private profit over economic fairness

(5) economic freedom over tyranny

55. Which of the situations described below *best* illustrates a violation of the Catholic bishops' view?

(1) Union Carbide, an American chemical company, operating a plant in Bhopal, India

(2) General Motors operating an automobile plant in Japan

(3) Coca Cola Company operating a bottling plant in Australia

(4) McDonald's permitting franchises to operate in Africa

(5) Ford Motor Company operating a plant in Canada

Questions 56–58 are based on the following passage.

The work which Jurgis was to do here was very simple, and it took him but a few minutes to learn it. He was provided with a stiff besom, such as is used by street sweepers, and it was his place to follow down the line the man who drew out the smoking entrails from the carcass of the steer; this mass was to be swept into a trap, which was then closed, so that no one might slip into it. As Jurgis came in, the first cattle of the morning were just making their appearance, and so, with scarcely time to look about him, and none to speak to anyone, he fell to work. It was a sweltering day in July, and the place ran with steaming hot blood—one waded in it on the floor. The stench was almost overpowering, but to Jurgis it was nothing. His whole soul was dancing with joy—he was at work at last! He was at work and earning money! All day long he was figuring to himself. He was paid the fabulous sum of seventeen and a half cents an hour, and as it proved a rush day and he worked until nearly seven o'clock in the evening, he went home to the family with the tidings that he had earned more than a dollar and a half in a single day!

56. Jurgis is employed as a

(1) worker in a slaughterhouse

(2) street sweeper

(3) hand on a ranch

(4) veterinarian's assistant

(5) skilled technician in a laboratory

57. The passage supports the fact that Jurgis

(1) is not a hard worker

(2) obtained the job through a friend

(3) needed special training for the job

(4) had been unemployed for a long time

(5) works alone

58. Jurgis is employed in the United States. In approximately what year is this story set?

(1) 1905

(2) 1945

(3) 1960

(4) 1970

(5) 1995

ANSWERS ARE ON PAGES 78-79.

Questions 59–61 are based on the information given about the following progressive reforms of the early twentieth century.

Sherman Anti-Trust Act—outlawed monopolies, including price-fixing and market-sharing

Hepburn Act—gave the Interstate Commerce Commission increased authority to regulate the nation's railroads

Pure Food and Drug Act—set standards for the production and sale of food and drugs

Child Labor Laws—put restrictions on the use of children in nonagricultural industries

U.S. Department of Agriculture—inspected meat and other foods to protect the public's health

59. What principle did *all* these reforms abandon completely?

   (1) *caveat emptor*—"let the buyer beware" before making a purchase
   (2) *laissez faire*—a belief that government should not interfere with business
   (3) *habeas corpus*—the requirement to bring an accused person to court to face charges
   (4) *social Darwinism*—the belief that the wealthy and powerful win in the battle for existence because of their biological superiority
   (5) *diminishing returns*—a situation in which the return on investment fails to increase in relation to additional investment

60. Which of the reforms established guidelines for testing products for the potential dangers of cancer-producing substances contained in them?

   (1) Sherman Anti-Trust Act
   (2) Hepburn Act
   (3) Pure Food and Drug Act
   (4) Child Labor Laws
   (5) U.S. Department of Agriculture

61. Which of the reforms prohibited the employment of a person under age fifteen who had received less than three months of schooling in the previous year?

   (1) Sherman Anti-Trust Act
   (2) Hepburn Act
   (3) Pure Food and Drug Act
   (4) Child Labor Laws
   (5) U.S. Department of Agriculture

62. Certain Baptists recently joined non-Christians in an effort to keep the State of Georgia from erecting a statue of Jesus along a highway. In taking such a stand, the Baptists were showing that they value

   (1) the right to privacy
   (2) free speech
   (3) their own personal freedom
   (4) the separation of church and state
   (5) the right to worship freely

ANSWERS ARE ON PAGE 79.

Political Science

Text pages 145–175

Question 1 is based on the following cartoon.

"How do I know what I think until I see how the opinion polls are going?"

1. The main idea of this cartoon is that some

   (1) candidates base their opinions on those of the voting public
   (2) voters decide how they will vote after reading the polls
   (3) media surveys attempt to influence the people being polled
   (4) managers of political campaigns do not believe in opinion polls
   (5) public opinion is influenced by popular political candidates

Questions 2 and 3 are based on the following passage.

Autumn 1987 signaled the beginning of Ronald Reagan's lame duck status as president. He was nearing the end of his second term; by law, he could not run again. His power and influence were diminishing with each new economic downfall, Soviet shove, or Mideast crisis. An article in the *Chicago Tribune* summed it up: "A long-time supporter and conservative Republican strategist used perhaps the unkindest words of all to describe any politician, especially a president. 'He's irrelevant,' the Republican said."

2. "Lame duck" status means a

   (1) position holding little command or prestige
   (2) rank of high influence
   (3) standing that is much hated and feared
   (4) condition of importance to only a few at the top
   (5) a state of constant controversy and turmoil

3. Which of the following presidents never entered lame duck status?

   (1) Jimmy Carter, who served from his defeat in November 1980 until Reagan's inauguration in 1981
   (2) Gerald Ford, who served after Nixon's resignation until Carter's swearing in
   (3) Lyndon Johnson, who withdrew from the 1968 race months before the election
   (4) John Kennedy, who was assassinated less than three years into his term
   (5) Dwight Eisenhower, who, before Reagan, was the last previous president to serve two full terms

ANSWERS ARE ON PAGE 79.

Questions 4–6 are based on the following passage.

Did you know that government can force U.S. citizens to sell their property? The right of **eminent domain** gives city, state, and federal government the power to take property from an owner if the seizure is done for a public purpose and if a fair price is offered. Governments have generally used eminent domain to acquire unsafe property that they wish to condemn or to acquire land for government projects.

In one unusual case, the California Supreme Court ruled that the City of Oakland could use the power of eminent domain to keep the Raiders from moving to Los Angeles. Higher courts later overturned that ruling on the grounds that football is not, primarily, a public activity.

Current debate over eminent domain mainly involves environmental regulations that severely limit how land can be used. These regulations do not take land from anyone, but government critics argue that something valuable has been taken nonetheless when developers are not allowed to build on their land or farmers are not allowed to drain their fields.

4. Which one of the following is an *improper* application of the right of eminent domain?

   (1) A city pays several homeowners the appraised market value of their houses in order to gain space for expansion of a school.
   (2) A city offers to purchase farmland at a fair price against an owner's wishes in order to build an airport.
   (3) A state buys land from a large corporation at a mutually agreed upon price in order to establish a state park.
   (4) A state pays a premium price for land it intends to resell to private parties later for a profit.
   (5) The federal government buys a huge tract of land from unwilling but well-paid sellers to extend a national park's boundaries.

5. What do the critics of environmental regulations regarding land use want the government to do?

   (1) exempt developers and farmers from environmental regulations
   (2) return the land taken by these regulations to the original owners
   (3) pay landowners for any decrease in their property value caused by regulation
   (4) eliminate all environmental regulations regarding how land is used
   (5) grant environmental groups ownership of the regulated lands

6. Which value are government officials allowing to take precedence when they apply their power of eminent domain?

   (1) the government's show of power over private ownership
   (2) the power of the federal over the local government
   (3) the welfare of a few over the financial concern of many
   (4) the public good over the rights of the individual
   (5) the private owners' rights over the public's pleasure

---

7. The system of checks and balances allows one branch of government to block actions by the other two branches. Which of the following actions involved use of the system of checks and balances?

   (1) Congress passing the Family and Medical Leave Act, which President Clinton supported
   (2) the Food and Drug Administration banning certain types of food labeling
   (3) President Bush pardoning six men involved in the Iran Contra affair
   (4) armed demonstrators preventing U.S. and Canadian troops from landing in Haiti
   (5) President Clinton dismissing the Director of the FBI because of alleged misconduct

ANSWERS ARE ON PAGE 79.

Questions 8–10 are based on the following constitutional amendments from the Bill of Rights:

First Amendment—guarantees the freedom of speech, religion, the press, and assembly

Second Amendment—guarantees the right to belong to a state militia and to bear arms

Fourth Amendment—requires presentation of a legal warrant before private property can be searched or seized

Sixth Amendment—guarantees the right to trial with a lawyer and by a jury in which witnesses against oneself can be seen and heard

Eighth Amendment—prohibits imposition of excessively high bail or cruel and unusual punishment

8. On the basis of which amendment is the death penalty often protested in the United States?

   (1) First
   (2) Second
   (3) Fourth
   (4) Sixth
   (5) Eighth

9. Because of its wording, which of the amendments is being used by some cities and other local governments to justify passing their own gun control laws?

   (1) First
   (2) Second
   (3) Fourth
   (4) Sixth
   (5) Eighth

10. A case is dismissed from traffic court because the witness to the accident does not show up. Upon which amendment is the dismissal based?

    (1) First
    (2) Second
    (3) Fourth
    (4) Sixth
    (5) Eighth

11. Many opponents of gun control legislation refer to a constitutional amendment to support their cause. Which of the following is the best *legal* argument in favor of gun control legislation?

    (1) Guns don't kill people; people kill people.
    (2) If everyone were armed, crime would automatically decrease tenfold.
    (3) The United States has a greater number of deaths caused by handguns than any other industrialized nation.
    (4) The right to bear arms applied only when colonial America had no standing army and armed citizens formed the militia.
    (5) Owners of handguns run a higher risk of having their weapons turned against them than those who don't own a gun.

12. A *lobby* is an organized group of people who actively seek to influence public opinion, policies, and actions. A lobby may be economic or social; however, its primary goal is to influence legislation favorable to its needs. Which of the following groups would *not* constitute a lobby?

    (1) International Brotherhood of Electrical Workers
    (2) a political action committee
    (3) the Ku Klux Klan
    (4) American Civil Liberties Union
    (5) International Ladies' Garment Workers Union

ANSWERS ARE ON PAGES 79–80.

Questions 13–15 are based on the following passage.

No person or branch of government in this country is required by law to keep the nation's budget balanced. The writers of the U.S. Constitution included many details to help guide a fair, flexible system of government into the twentieth century, but they could not have anticipated the fiscal irresponsibility exhibited by our government officials over the past several years.

13. Which of the following restates an opinion of the author of this passage?

(1) The U.S. Constitution does not provide for a balanced budget.
(2) The U.S. Constitution has endured into the twentieth century.
(3) Congress cannot be blamed for the budgetary crisis in the United States today.
(4) The President of the United States should be the one to balance the budget.
(5) U.S. government officials are to blame for the huge budget deficit.

14. Which of the following hypotheses would the author of the above passage most likely support?

(1) Balancing the nation's budget is not possible today.
(2) Keeping the country's budget balanced is not fiscally wise.
(3) Reduced Congressional spending would not help balance the budget today.
(4) Hiring economic consultants to balance the budget is now necessary.
(5) Adding a constitutional amendment to require a balanced budget might solve the problem.

15. Which of the following is the best argument *against* passing a balanced budget amendment?

(1) The amendment process would be too costly because of the legal expertise needed to draft an amendment.
(2) The amendment process would take too long to do the country any good.
(3) The Constitution is sacred and was not meant to be tampered with in such a trivial way.
(4) If American citizens must live within their means, so should the American government.
(5) A balanced budget amendment might prevent the government from obtaining needed money during national emergencies.

Questions 16 and 17 are based on the following passage.

Freedom to say and write what we want, when we want, is something Americans assume we will always have. We believe that such freedom is a basic human right, not to be denied us by any person or government.

Such freedom is not always granted in communist Vietnam, however. Some freedoms have been granted in recent years. Under Vietnam's version of glasnost, called *doi moi* (renovation), writers and filmmakers now discuss light, romantic themes instead of stories of heroic Marxist struggle. However, the government is quick to suppress speech that might undermine its authority, especially the speech of religious leaders. Officials in Hanoi have censored sermons, forced monks and priests to participate in propaganda campaigns, and jailed religious leaders.

16. The writer implies that freedom of speech is

(1) something not taken for granted by Vietnamese citizens
(2) something taken for granted too often by citizens of all countries
(3) a right that U.S. citizens cannot be denied, no matter what they say
(4) a right that citizens of all countries are granted under special circumstances
(5) a privilege that should only be restricted when citizens threaten the government

ANSWERS ARE ON PAGE 80.

17. Which of the following statements about *doi moi* is adequately supported by this paragraph? Under *doi moi*,

  (1) Vietnamese citizens can speak and write without restrictions.
  (2) writers and filmmakers are restricted to political topics.
  (3) government leaders are granting freedoms formerly restricted in Vietnam.
  (4) Vietnamese leaders are granting fewer freedoms to citizens than ever before.
  (5) Vietnamese citizens now have the freedom to participate in political campaigns.

Questions 18 and 19 are based on the following newspaper article.

In Lake County, Illinois, the state's attorney is expected to re-indict a convicted murderer whose sentencing was reversed by the state supreme court. A Lake County jury found the convicted felon guilty but mentally ill in a case involving the stabbing of a teenager. The high court upheld an appeals court decision that the defendant should have been found not guilty by reason of insanity.

The state's attorney challenged the appeals court ruling, accusing the judges of acting as a "thirteenth juror." These judges had decided that the jury should have given more weight to the defense witness's testimony than that of the prosecution's witness when the jury sought to determine the killer's state of mental health at the time of the killing.

The state supreme court upheld the appellate decision, declaring that a new trial on the same charge would not be appropriate because it would violate the defendant's protection against double jeopardy (the constitutional rule that a person cannot be tried twice for the same crime).

In making his case for a second trial, the state's attorney will introduce a Florida case, which may bring about a review of the Illinois case by the U.S. Supreme Court. In the Florida case, a higher court ruled that when a conviction is overturned based on credibility of witnesses, a second trial is warranted.

18. The Lake County state's attorney intends to use the decision in a Florida case to convince the U.S. Supreme Court to review the case. The citing of an earlier, similar case in order to attain the desired legal decision in another is referred to as citing a legal

  (1) appeal
  (2) precedent
  (3) license
  (4) loophole
  (5) statute

19. Which one of the following statements is *not* adequately supported by information in the article?

  (1) The defendant was freed because of the finding that he was not guilty by reason of insanity.
  (2) The state's attorney charged that the appellate court had overstepped its bounds when it ruled against the jury's decision.
  (3) The defendant was a minor but was tried as an adult.
  (4) All parties agree that the defendant was mentally ill but not that he should be sentenced for his actions.
  (5) When the defendant is mentally ill, courts give significant weight to how believable a witness is when determining a defendant's rights.

ANSWERS ARE ON PAGE 80.

Questions 20 and 21 are based on the following graph.

SATISFACTION WITH GOVERNMENT SPENDING

From which level of government do you feel you get the most for your money--federal, state or local?

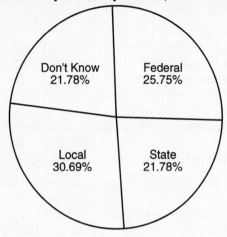

Don't Know 21.78%

Federal 25.75%

Local 30.69%

State 21.78%

20. According to the results of this survey, a U.S. citizen would be most likely to support spending controls on which body?

(1) Congress
(2) Legislature
(3) Mayor's office
(4) the White House
(5) the School Board

21. Which factor probably contributes most to people's approval of local spending over federal?

(1) scandals in the personal lives of federal officials
(2) politically inexperienced government officials
(3) reports of failure in the public school system
(4) politician's use of expensive media campaigns while running for office
(5) highly visible local programs, such as street and highway work

Questions 22–24 are based on the following terms.

radical—one who advocates sweeping changes in laws and methods of government with the least delay

liberal—one who advocates political change in the name of progress, especially social improvement through governmental action

moderate—one who believes in avoiding extreme changes and measures in laws and government

conservative—one who advocates maintaining the existing social order under a strict interpretation of the Constitution

reactionary—one who resists change and usually advocates a return to an earlier social order or policy

22. In an election, the winning candidate, the incumbent, attributed her success to her popularity in small towns and rural areas where people were comfortable with the status quo and favored little or no change. The voters in those villages and on those farms could be described as politically

(1) radical
(2) liberal
(3) moderate
(4) conservative
(5) reactionary

23. Groups of students who were bitterly opposed to the present government and its Constitution staged rallies and marches to protest the victory of the incumbent in hopes of getting a new election immediately. These students are politically

(1) radical
(2) liberal
(3) moderate
(4) conservative
(5) reactionary

24. The incumbent candidate had two opponents. Both opponents proposed reforming welfare programs, national medical policies, and agriculture. Both candidates were considered politically

(1) radical
(2) liberal
(3) moderate
(4) conservative
(5) reactionary

ANSWERS ARE ON PAGE 80.

Questions 25–27 are based on the following passage.

Will business as usual continue in Hong Kong? With the expiration of the British lease on the colony, this, the most efficient of business communities, becomes part of communist China. Under the terms of the Sino-British exit agreement, Hong Kong maintains control over its own commercial and domestic affairs for 50 years. However, many Hong Kong residents, often refugees from the mainland, do not trust the communists, and so they flee.

25. From the passage, you can infer that before the recent change in power Hong Kong was controlled by

   (1) refugees
   (2) Great Britain
   (3) Taiwan
   (4) local residents
   (5) businessmen

26. What probably makes Hong Kong residents fear communist control the most?

   (1) the threat of competition from Chinese businesses
   (2) chronic instability in the Chinese government
   (3) China's past history of human rights violations
   (4) the threat that the communists will use military force to seize control
   (5) racial differences between communist rulers and Hong Kong residents

27. The passage implies that the most immediate threat to Hong Kong may be from

   (1) British imperialism
   (2) flight of professional talent from the city
   (3) Communist control of the economy
   (4) Communist restrictions in local politics
   (5) loss of natural resources

Questions 28 and 29 are based on the following passage.

George Washington was in a unique position. He was the first president and the only one to not have been elected within a political party system. By 1800, however, the third presidential election had made clear the need for a constitutional amendment. The Twelfth Amendment declared essentially that candidates for president and vice president must run together on the same ticket. In previous presidential elections, the office of the vice presidency had been given to the second-highest vote-getter in the general election.

28. The biggest problem with the original system of selecting the vice president of the United States was that

   (1) two or more candidates for president could receive the same number of votes
   (2) the president and vice president could be of opposing political viewpoints
   (3) perhaps none of the presidential candidates would desire the office of the vice presidency
   (4) the electors might not want the second-highest vote-getter as vice president
   (5) one presidential candidate could receive all of the electoral votes

29. As a result of the Twelfth Amendment, at the political conventions now held before presidential elections, political parties

   (1) select several presidential candidates to run in the national election later
   (2) select the presidential and vice presidential candidates most popular with the delegates
   (3) select the highest vote-getter as the presidential candidate and the second highest as the vice presidential candidate
   (4) select a presidential candidate who then picks a vice presidential running-mate
   (5) select their presidential and vice presidential candidates in separate votes

ANSWERS ARE ON PAGES 80-81.

Question 30 is based on the following graph.

TAX DOLLARS WASTED
Which government wastes the most of your tax dollar?

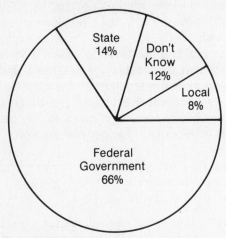

Source: the Waukegan (Ill.) *News-Sun*, Nov. 1, 1987

30. Which of the following statements can be adequately supported by the information given in the graph?

(1) People may not think the federal income tax is fair, but they do not blame federal officials.

(2) People may not like state sales and income taxes, but they do not blame state officials for them.

(3) People may not like local property taxes, but they like the federal income tax even less.

(4) The majority of people think federal dollars are wasted, but they still trust federal officials.

(5) Though many people responded "Don't know" to the question, they can be counted as agreeing with the majority.

---

31. The saying "Nothing in life is certain except death and taxes" means that

(1) the American people are being taxed to death

(2) the heirs of the dead who owned real estate must pay inheritance taxes

(3) as surely as people will die one day, they will always pay taxes when alive

(4) there always have been taxes and there will always be taxes

(5) certain people can escape paying taxes, but they can't escape death

32. The retail sales tax, first enacted by Mississippi in 1932, spread to many states as a way of raising needed revenue. So widespread is the sales tax today that few of the 50 states do not have one. Which of the following characteristics of the sales tax does *not* contribute directly to its popularity?

(1) Collection is painless because it is taken in small amounts.

(2) The sales tax meets with less opposition than do other kinds of taxes.

(3) Administration of the tax is easy because tax returns are unnecessary.

(4) The retail sales tax is perceived to be a fair tax.

(5) Larger families pay more sales tax than smaller families.

33. A weakness of the sales tax is that low-income persons pay a higher percentage of their income in taxes than do wealthy persons. Which of the following types of taxes would help reduce this unfair aspect of the retail sales tax?

(1) an excise tax on alcoholic beverages

(2) a luxury tax on luxury cars, furs, and other costly items

(3) an excise tax on cigarettes and tobacco products

(4) a tax on motor fuel

(5) an excise tax on public utility services

34. A sales tax on which of the following items would be considered *most* unfair for the poor?

(1) shelter

(2) clothing

(3) food

(4) cigarettes

(5) public utility services

ANSWERS ARE ON PAGE 81.

Questions 35–38 are based on the passage below.

An **estate** is a social or political class vested with distinct political powers. The traditional parliamentary estate originated in France around the fourteenth century and was called the "Estates General." The purpose of this body was to give counsel and support to a king who had to make decisions for the nation.

Three estates were recognized and were considered to represent the will and desire of three groups. The First Estate represented the clergy; the Second Estate, the nobility or titled class; and the Third Estate, the common people.

Years later, a Fourth Estate, the public press, was recognized as a distinct power with an enormous impact on the decision-making process, particularly in a democracy such as ours. In the United States today we often refer to the four parts of the body politic as estates.

35. The main idea of the passage is that estates

    (1) were created in France in the fourteenth century and are still functioning today
    (2) represented the will of the people
    (3) were political divisions that once served a distinct purpose in government
    (4) were never a formal part of the U.S. governmental system
    (5) are the forerunners of the American democratic system

36. Which of the following could be classified *best* as belonging to the Fourth Estate?

    (1) a political action committee
    (2) the American Broadcasting Company
    (3) an English nobleman
    (4) the *National Enquirer*
    (5) the American Civil Liberties Union

37. The Estates General could not have been adopted and used successfully by a president of the United States because

    (1) only the common people's voices count in America
    (2) our Constitution does not permit titles of nobility to be granted
    (3) the American press has too much power
    (4) presidents rely only on the advice of their cabinet members
    (5) the clergy has no real political authority in the United States

38. Which of the following is another good reason why the Estates General as an advisory body could not have been adopted by the United States?

    (1) The people in a democracy have too much political power.
    (2) The Estates General can be applied only to a monarchy.
    (3) The U.S. government was founded on the principle of separation of church and state.
    (4) The wealthy class replaced the nobility in the United States.
    (5) The assembly that was made up of the three estates outlived its usefulness.

Question 39 is based on the following quote from the United States Constitution.

No person shall be a Senator who shall not have attained the age of thirty years, and been nine years a citizen of the United States, and who shall not, when elected, be an inhabitant of that State for which he shall be chosen.

39. Which of the following people would *not* be qualified to run for senator of the United States from the state of Oregon?

    (1) a thirty-year-old woman who is a lifelong resident of Beaverton, Oregon
    (2) a sixty-five-year-old retired native Oregonian who has moved to Florida
    (3) a forty-two-year-old Russian immigrant who has lived in Oregon since he became a naturalized citizen at age 30
    (4) an eighty-year-old widow, born in Iowa but settled in Oregon since 1940
    (5) a fifty-three-year-old native of Texas who moved to Oregon six months ago

ANSWERS ARE ON PAGE 81.

Questions 40–43 are based on the following passage.

Approximately 170 countries exist today, and about 160 of them have constitutions based directly or indirectly on the United States model. Japan's, drafted with much American influence right after World War II, contains the unusual stipulation that Japan will never again wage war against other countries or even maintain an army, navy, or air force. Not all national charters have been as heavily dominated by the ideas or desires of the United States, however. In fact, most countries constantly rewrite their constitutions or ignore major principles in them in order to fit the political inclination of the current ruler.

40. The Japanese spend only about 1 percent of their gross national product on defense because they

(1) are dominated by American influences
(2) have never engaged in a war
(3) owe so much money to the United States
(4) still have expenses from World War I
(5) do not pay for armed services

41. Because of the fears of the return of dictatorships in Germany and Italy after World War I, the framers of their constitutions severely limited the

(1) power of the executive branch
(2) number of representatives in Parliament
(3) court system
(4) amendment process
(5) rights of individuals

42. With which of the following opinions would the writer of the passage most likely agree?

(1) The United States should follow the example set by other countries that have changed constitutions about every 20 years.
(2) The use of the United States Constitution as a model has led to problems of misinterpretation of its principles in other countries.
(3) The United States Constitution is a unique document that has had a wide-ranging influence on politics around the world.
(4) Japan's constitution should be used as the model for other countries because of its rule against waging war.
(5) Americans were too harsh in their demand that Japan give up its support of an army, navy, and air force.

43. China's current constitution grants freedom of speech, the press, assembly, association, procession, and demonstration. Which one of the following actions by the Peking government directly contradicted one of the freedoms listed?

(1) loosening the regulations about who could enter the country
(2) shutting down production of several liberal periodicals
(3) allowing some movies to be made there by Westerners
(4) discouraging Buddhist religious festivals at the new year
(5) maintaining strict control over the limited court system

ANSWERS ARE ON PAGE 81.

Questions 44–46 are based on the following map.

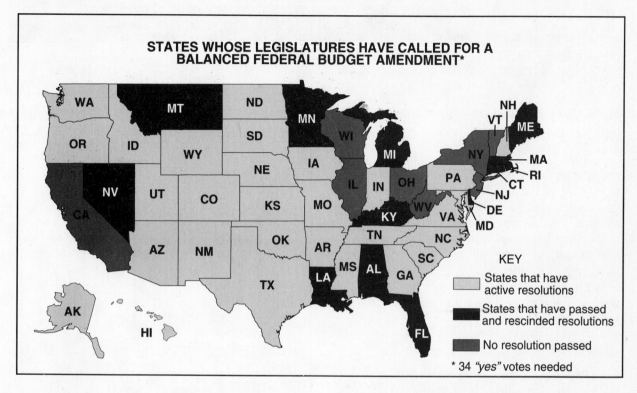

STATES WHOSE LEGISLATURES HAVE CALLED FOR A BALANCED FEDERAL BUDGET AMENDMENT*

KEY

States that have active resolutions

States that have passed and rescinded resolutions

No resolution passed

* 34 *"yes"* votes needed

44. According to this map, which one of the following states voted for a constitutional convention, but later withdrew its approval?

(1) Louisiana
(2) California
(3) New York
(4) Pennsylvania
(5) Wisconsin

45. Which of the following facts about the amendment process is adequately supported by information given in the map?

(1) Two-thirds of the state legislatures must call for the national convention in order for it to take place.
(2) The ability of a state legislature to revoke its positive vote for a convention is being debated.
(3) An alternate method of amending the Constitution is for Congress to introduce the idea and vote it in.
(4) The method of the states calling for a convention usually takes many years of debates and votes.
(5) Political action groups for and against an amendment work hard in every state that is shown as undecided.

46. More than 10,000 amendments to the Constitution have been proposed in Congress since 1789, but just twenty-six of them have won both the approval of two-thirds of the houses of Congress and the adoption by three-fourths of the state legislatures. Such statistics give testament to the fact that the framers of the United States Constitution

(1) did not anticipate the need for change in a legal document that would last generations
(2) planned that any changes in the Constitution allowed by the amendment process would be fundamental and important
(3) wanted the amendment process to be easy so that changes could be made frequently
(4) thought that the Constitution was complete as written and did not need to be added to
(5) looked at the amendment process in other constitutions before drafting the one in use

ANSWERS ARE ON PAGES 81–82.

Behavioral Sciences

Text pages
177–209

Questions 1 and 2 are based on the following quote.

When I'm in a fire camp I look around and try to find a woman who's forty years old or thirty-five or fifty, like all the men I see. I want to see a woman who's walking around not just in a fire camp, but on the fire line. I've never seen her. And that really bothers me because I want to see her. I realize the role model has to be myself. I'm going to be the role model for other people, and that's one of the reasons why, even when my job was less than I wanted, I stuck it out. I want to be that woman on the fire line.

1. Diana Clarke has concluded that

   (1) fighting fires is too difficult for women above the age of thirty-five
   (2) fire-fighting jobs that women can perform are too scarce to bother seeking
   (3) presently, women are not allowed to work as firefighters past age thirty-five
   (4) in the past, women did not actively pursue firefighting as a career
   (5) in the future, women will not be as motivated to seek jobs as firefighters

2. When Diana Clarke says she will be a role model in the future, she is implying that

   (1) other women will use her career as an example to follow
   (2) more men and women will seek firefighting as a career
   (3) most people will not take her or her career seriously
   (4) many men's careers will be threatened by the advances in hers
   (5) people will think of firefighting as more for women than for men

Questions 3 and 4 are based on the following cartoon.

"Jim claims it triples their attention span."

3. The man behind the television screen is a

   (1) college math teacher
   (2) junior high school teacher
   (3) school administrator
   (4) television performer
   (5) guest in the school

4. The cartoon supports the belief that children

   (1) have little respect for teachers these days
   (2) can enjoy high level thinking if they are pushed to do so
   (3) are more attentive when watching TV than when listening to a teacher
   (4) are less attentive to TV than to a person talking to them directly
   (5) need variety and entertainment in the classroom in order to learn

ANSWERS ARE ON PAGE 82.

Questions 5–7 are based on the following passage.

The Pacific man does not see the ocean as implacable and hostile. He is incapable of weeping on the beach as do Portuguese fisher folk when their boats put out. He has none of the dread of the sea that is found in the bittersweet regard of the Scotch and the New Englanders. The Pacific man sees the ocean as Olympian . . . outsized and majestic, capable of enormous power, but also capable of foolishness and mistakes. It gives his life all the tension it needs.

There is, I think, a reason for this. Throughout Oceania, in the great archipelagoes with their vast sweeps of salt water and their tiny specks of islands, men have not yet dominated nature. Nature is lived with gingerly, delicately, sometimes with zest and daring, but always with awe and sometimes with a crawling eerie fear. Not having mastered nature, the man of Oceania has little desire to master other men. His art, his politics, his manners, his religion, his industry all seem miniature and bleached and diminished because of a looming presence: the Pacific.

5. Which of the following theories is supported by the passage above?

  (1) Development of a culture is affected by the natural environment in which it grows.
  (2) Primitive civilizations have developed better control over nature than more advanced ones.
  (3) Populations that depend on the sea for livelihood are less sophisticated culturally than those that do not.
  (4) The structure of a society is determined by the race of its inhabitants.
  (5) The people of a region are as dangerous to other people as nature has been to them.

6. Considering the information given in the passage about Pacific islanders, it can be concluded that they

  (1) are not willing to become westernized
  (2) have complicated music, dances, and legends in their culture
  (3) have accepted Christianity on most islands
  (4) are sexually freer than Europeans
  (5) seldom become involved in wars

7. In their outlook toward nature, the Pacific islanders most resemble

  (1) Eastern Europeans
  (2) South Americans
  (3) Native Americans
  (4) Orientals
  (5) Canadians

Questions 8 and 9 are based on the following passage.

You'd love Peter. He's a real charmer. He speaks with a wonderful Hungarian accent and lives in beautiful comfort on a hill overlooking his adopted city of Vienna. He is now in his eighties and as alert and challenging as a teenager. He has a most fascinating philosophy. He observes that people seem to live life in three states: the state of *must*, the state of *should*, and the state of *want to*. Happiness according to Peter is determined by how much of our lives is spent in the state of *want to*.

8. Which of the following situations would Peter value most highly?

  (1) taking time from a busy day for a walk in the park
  (2) attending a class required for job advancement by an employer
  (3) going for a checkup to a dentist every six months
  (4) making a healthy dinner every night at 6:00
  (5) writing thank-you notes after receiving presents for a special occasion

9. With which of the following statements would Peter most likely agree?

  (1) People who spend most of their lives wanting to do things should face reality.
  (2) People who fulfill certain responsibilities because they have to are always unhappy.
  (3) People who fulfill certain responsibilities because they *should* do them are guilt-driven.
  (4) People who are daring and who do many exciting things live life to the fullest.
  (5) People who take risks are foolhardy.

ANSWERS ARE ON PAGE 82.

Questions 10–12 are based on the following survey results in response to the question "What is your main religious affiliation?"

INVOLVEMENT IN RELIGIOUS GROUPS

	1985	1993
Protestant	62.5% (955)	64.2% (1026)
Catholic	26.7% (408)	22.0% (351)
Jewish	2.1% (32)	2.1% (33)
None	7.1% (109)	9.1% (146)
Other	1.6% (25)	2.6% (42)
Total	*100% (1529)*	*100% (1598)*

10. Which group grew the most between 1985 and 1993?

   (1) Protestant
   (2) Catholic
   (3) Jewish
   (4) None
   (5) Other

11. In which group did participation decline between 1985 and 1993?

   (1) Protestant
   (2) Catholic
   (3) Jewish
   (4) None
   (5) Other

12. Which statement do these survey results support?

   (1) Americans are more involved in religious movements than ever before.
   (2) The rise in Protestant membership occurred mostly in fundamentalist denominations.
   (3) Protestant church members are attending services more often than ever before.
   (4) Assimilation is threatening the future of the Jewish community in America.
   (5) American involvement in nontraditional religions is on the rise.

13. *Acculturation* is the process of acquiring the dominant culture of an area other than one's birth and upbringing. Which of the following situations *best* illustrates the concept of acculturation?

   (1) American grade-school pupils learning to speak Latin
   (2) suburban California housewives learning to cook Cajun foods
   (3) Indian immigrants to America continuing to wear their native dress
   (4) Puerto Ricans in New York resisting speaking English
   (5) Vietnamese refugees to the United States learning to eat with forks

14. One's *ascribed status* is the position a person inherits through birth or attains with age; one's *achieved status* is the position a person attains through individual effort. Which of the following is considered an ascribed status?

   (1) taxpayer
   (2) priest
   (3) bookworm
   (4) Duke of Windsor
   (5) beauty queen

15. Which of the following is considered an achieved status?

   (1) identical twin
   (2) adolescent
   (3) most valuable player
   (4) heiress
   (5) retiree

16. A psychologist states that neurotic and psychotic individuals have not learned to use defense mechanisms to reduce their conflicts and frustrations. The psychologist is implying that

   (1) only the mentally ill experience conflicts and frustrations
   (2) the use of defense mechanisms can be healthy
   (3) the mentally ill have a reduced capacity for learning
   (4) neurotics and psychotics need to avoid the use of defense mechanisms
   (5) defense mechanisms do not help reduce conflicts and frustrations

ANSWERS ARE ON PAGE 82.

Questions 17–20 are based on the following terms.

primary group—a group in which the members share highly personal relationships

secondary group—a group in which the members work together for a common purpose but do not share close personal relationships

institution—a system organized by society to provide for its members' family, religious, political, economic, and educational needs

nuclear family—a group consisting of a mother, father, and children who live in the same household

extended family—a group composed of family members beyond the immediate members of mother, father, and children, all of whom live in the same household

17. Which of the following terms would a sociologist apply to volunteers who band together to help victims of a flood?

    (1) primary group
    (2) secondary group
    (3) institution
    (4) nuclear family
    (5) extended family

18. Which of the following terms would a sociologist use to describe a group living together and consisting of a divorced father, his son and daughter, his mother, and his brother?

    (1) primary group
    (2) secondary group
    (3) institution
    (4) nuclear family
    (5) extended family

19. Which of the following terms would a sociologist apply to the Lutheran Church in the United States?

    (1) primary group
    (2) secondary group
    (3) institution
    (4) nuclear family
    (5) extended family

20. What would a sociologist call you and your two closest friends?

    (1) primary group
    (2) secondary group
    (3) institution
    (4) nuclear family
    (5) extended family

Questions 21 and 22 are based on the following passage.

Because of an extreme population explosion, the government of the People's Republic of China has forbidden mothers to bear more than one child. As a result of this policy, another problem has arisen, described as the "four-two-one syndrome," in which four grandparents and two parents have assumed the responsibility for one child. These only children have been labeled "little emperors" by the Chinese press, which echoes everyone's fears that the children are growing up to be lazy, spoiled, and self-centered.

21. The "four-two-one" syndrome might possibly be cured if

    (1) the press gave voice to everyone's fears about the children becoming "little emperors"
    (2) Chinese couples refused to have any children at all
    (3) the Chinese government revoked the ban against large families
    (4) Chinese children were sent to school at an earlier age
    (5) Chinese grandparents had no contact with their grandchildren

22. By calling Chinese only children "little emperors," the Chinese press implies that

    (1) everyone fears the children, just as they do dictators
    (2) the children are wealthy, like kings and queens
    (3) the children are treated like royalty by their parents
    (4) their attitude is old-fashioned and inappropriate
    (5) they are not being allowed to grow up like children

ANSWERS ARE ON PAGE 83.

Questions 23 and 24 are based on the following chart.

MASLOW'S HIERARCHY OF HUMAN NEEDS

Need for Self-Actualization

Esteem Needs

Belongingness Needs

Safety and Security Needs

Physiological (Survival) Needs

Before you can experience love, you must feel safe, secure, and nourished. So says psychologist Abraham Maslow in his theory of a succeeding level of needs, shown graphically above.

23. Which of the following statements is adequately supported by Maslow's theory?

(1) Before you can feel safe, you must feel like you are part of a group.

(2) Before you can feel admiration from co-workers, you must feel part of the group.

(3) Before you can experience love at home, you must feel respect on the job.

(4) Before you can feel part of a group, you must feel honored by its members.

(5) Before you can feel sheltered and secure, you must feel that you belong to a group.

24. Other theorists have set up models similar to Maslow's. Which one of the following model terms is most like *self-actualization*, the highest need, which is the need to fully realize one's potential?

(1) *individuation*—the need to appreciate one's place in human history

(2) *gratification*—the fulfillment of a need or needs

(3) *frustration*—a need that is unfulfilled or produces conflict

(4) *rationalization*—the need to assign blame to other than the true cause of a problem

(5) *socialization*—the process needed to assimilate an individual into society

Questions 25 and 26 are based on the excerpt below.

Although some accommodations are being made to changing family structures, the bottom line of the message remains clear to anyone who has lived through it—the normal mother, the caring mother, the *good* mother, is at home. Ask any working parent who's tried to find a pediatrician at 7:00 A.M. or 9:00 P.M. Ask anyone who's tried to make special arrangements for appliance servicing or child care on school vacation days. Ask a parent who's tried to find adequate day care for an infant or preschooler. Many people believe that times have changed in the past few years and that women's (and men's) roles are different and more flexible. But as far as substantive, *real* changes in provisions for families with working mothers are concerned, there has been little more than rhetoric. Ask any working mother. Or father for that matter.

25. The main point of this excerpt is that

(1) pediatricians should be more accommodating to working parents

(2) mothers should not work outside the home

(3) children have suffered in the changing family structures

(4) society has not changed to provide for new family situations

(5) fathers should take on more domestic responsibilities these days

26. This excerpt supports the inference that, according to the larger society, working mothers

(1) neglect their children

(2) value their jobs over their children's welfare

(3) are responsible for increased juvenile delinquency

(4) are treated unfairly

(5) fall short in those areas that define a good mother

ANSWERS ARE ON PAGE 83.

Questions 27–30 are based on the following graph.

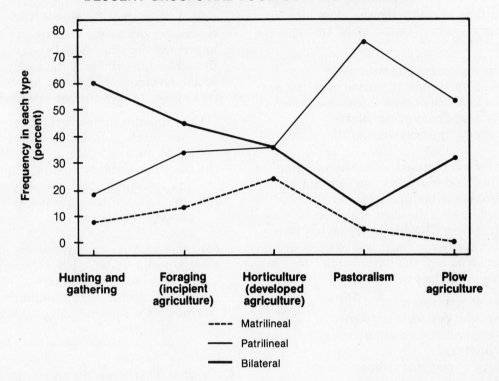

DESCENT GROUPS AND FOOD-GETTING METHODS

---- Matrilineal

—— Patrilineal

—— Bilateral

27. *Matrilineal, patrilineal,* and *bilateral* refer to lines of descent— the way the family's line is seen to pass. It may pass through the mother (*matri*), the father (*patri*), or combination (*bi*).

According to the graph, the food-getting method most *rarely* used by the matrilineal type of society is

(1) hunting and gathering
(2) foraging
(3) horticulture
(4) pastoralism
(5) plow agriculture

28. The food-getting method used most frequently by the bilateral type of family is

(1) hunting and gathering
(2) foraging
(3) horticulture
(4) pastoralism
(5) plow agriculture

29. The food-getting method used equally by bilateral and patrilineal societies is

(1) hunting and gathering
(2) foraging
(3) horticulture
(4) pastoralism
(5) plow agriculture

30. According to the graph, the more advanced the means of food-getting, the

(1) lower the number of children in a family
(2) greater the number of single-parent families
(3) fewer the number of farmers in a society
(4) easier it is to trace the family line through the mother
(5) greater the chance of tracing family lines through the fathers

ANSWERS ARE ON PAGE 83.

Questions 31 and 32 are based on the following hypothesis.

According to psychologists, most men who abuse their wives have certain traits. Among these traits are

- poor self-image and insecurity
- stereotyped views of women as subservient
- repeated violent experiences in childhood
- lack of ability to communicate
- economic pressures due to little income

31. Martha is a battered wife. She says that her husband is a good provider, but he never talks to her and treats her like his maid. She says she stays with him because she feels sorry for him since he has little respect for himself and was abused by his father. Which of the named traits does *not* apply to Martha's husband?

(1) poor self-image
(2) stereotyped view of women
(3) repeated violent experiences in childhood
(4) lack of communication
(5) economic pressures

32. The well-documented fact that spouse abuse cuts across all salary levels seems to contradict the theory of psychologists that abusers act out of

(1) poor self-image
(2) stereotyped view of women
(3) repeated violent experiences in childhood
(4) lack of communication
(5) economic pressures

33. A study of inmate records at a major U.S. prison reveals that most inmates did not finish school and most did poorly in school when they did attend. The researcher draws the conclusion that improving the educational system in the United States will lower the high rate of social deviation. In drawing his conclusion, the researcher assumed that

(1) the inmates did not get along with their teachers and, therefore, had problems in schools
(2) there is no way at present to improve an increasingly bad school system
(3) attendance at school is not as important as doing well in the subject areas
(4) other factors, such as home environment, were not the primary cause of social deviation
(5) school records were kept on the prison inmates who were being studied

34. *Cultural diffusion* is the spreading of cultural elements of one society into another—for example, American-style fast-food restaurants that spring up in such far away places as Sydney, Australia; Bangkok, Thailand; and Paris, France. Which of the following is another example of cultural diffusion?

(1) the persistence of Pacific Islanders in making bark cloth despite the accessibility of polyesters and cottons
(2) the predominance of Buddhism among Asians and Judaism and Christianity among Europeans
(3) the tendency among immigrants to the United States to adopt American ways and lose their own
(4) the expansion of American rock music to all parts of the globe
(5) the development of international groups dedicated to aiding poor, starving countries

ANSWERS ARE ON PAGE 83.

Questions 35 and 36 are based on the following terms from theories of learning known as behaviorism.

shaping—a desired behavior is taught by rewarding even partially correct responses to stimuli

discrimination training—a desired behavior is taught by rewarding only correct responses to particular stimuli

avoidance conditioning—a particular behavior is taught to be avoided by punishing its occurrence

extinction—a previously learned behavior is eliminated by no longer presenting the stimuli that produced it

reconditioning—an extinct behavior is retaught by presenting the stimuli that originally brought out the response

35. When a parent spanks a child for running out into the street, he or she is using

    (1) shaping
    (2) discrimination training
    (3) avoidance conditioning
    (4) extinction
    (5) reconditioning

36. When a supervisor praises a secretary for typing a letter despite several misspellings and the need to retype it, that supervisor is training the employee through

    (1) shaping
    (2) discrimination training
    (3) avoidance conditioning
    (4) extinction
    (5) reconditioning

Questions 37 and 38 are based on the following chart.

DISTRIBUTION OF A, B, AND O BLOOD TYPES IN SELECTED ETHNIC GROUPS
(in percent)

	O	A	B	AB
Native Americans	97.4	2.6		
Australian Aborigines	48.1	51.9		
Basques	57.2	41.7		
English	47.9	42.4	8.3	1.4
Black Americans	51.5	29.5	15.5	3.5
White Americans	42.2	39.3	13.5	5.1
Chinese	30.7	25.1	34.2	10.0
Asian Indians	32.5	20.0	39.4	8.1

37. Many anthropologists believe that Native Americans, who primarily have type O blood, migrated to North America from Asia, where type B is most commonly found. The facts in the chart seem to refute the anthropologists' theory because

    A. Chinese and Asian Indians have a much lower proportion of members with type O blood

    B. Native Americans have no members with type B blood

    C. Asian Indians and the Chinese have a similar distribution of blood types across their two ethnic groups

    (1) A only
    (2) B only
    (3) C only
    (4) A and B
    (5) A and C

38. Based on the information about the blood type of nearly all Native Americans, which is the most reasonable hypothesis about why type O blood predominates?

    (1) Type B is inferior to type O blood.
    (2) Type A is not suited to the environmental conditions of North America.
    (3) Type O is superior to all other blood types.
    (4) Type O emerged through a biological process similar to natural selection.
    (5) Type AB was bred out of Native Americans over a period of thousands of years.

ANSWERS ARE ON PAGES 83-84.

Questions 39–42 are based on the following terms that psychologists apply to defense mechanisms used to ward off anxiety.

rationalization—disguising the real reason for one's failure to reach a goal

repression—keeping unpleasant thoughts that cause anxiety hidden in one's subconscious

projection—assigning a bad trait or problem of one's own to another person

displacement—transferring one's frustration to a person or object that did not cause it

reaction formation—behaving in a way opposite to one's beliefs or feelings

39. Al did not have a happy childhood but will not talk about it. He says he does not remember very much of it. Al is using the defense mechanism of

    (1) rationalization
    (2) repression
    (3) projection
    (4) displacement
    (5) reaction formation

40. Marie is in love with James but cannot admit it to herself or James. Instead, she pretends as if she hardly notices him and does not care to know him. Marie is using the defense mechanism known as

    (1) rationalization
    (2) repression
    (3) projection
    (4) displacement
    (5) reaction formation

41. Jack stays out all night partying and fails to complete an important homework assignment. When the teacher confronts him about it, he complains that the assignment was too boring to hold his interest. Jack is using the defense mechanism known as

    (1) rationalization
    (2) repression
    (3) projection
    (4) displacement
    (5) reaction formation

42. Paranoia is a personality disorder in which its victims are highly suspicious of others and believe that people are plotting against them. Paranoia could be described as an extreme form of

    (1) rationalization
    (2) repression
    (3) projection
    (4) displacement
    (5) reaction formation

Questions 43 and 44 are based on the five steps in the scientific method that scientists follow to ensure objectivity in conducting experiments.

STEP 1—observing a problem

STEP 2—developing a theory (hypothesis) about the problem

STEP 3—designing an experiment or carrying out research to prove or disprove the theory

STEP 4—carrying out the experiment and summarizing the findings

STEP 5—drawing conclusions from the findings and verifying the conclusions through more experiments

43. A psychologist who supposes that her chronically depressed clients might be helped by adopting pets would be

    (1) observing a problem
    (2) developing a theory
    (3) designing an experiment
    (4) carrying out the experiment
    (5) drawing conclusions

44. After pairing pets with half her depressed patients, the psychologist decides that pets do indeed help such people cope with anxiety and will continue trying it with other patients. The step this psychologist has reached is

    (1) observing a problem
    (2) developing a theory
    (3) designing an experiment
    (4) carrying out the experiment
    (5) drawing conclusions

ANSWERS ARE ON PAGE 84.

Questions 45–47 are based on the following passage.

In December of 1986, a group of researchers at the University of Minnesota announced results of a study of 350 pairs of identical twins reared apart. In more than half of the cases studied they found that the tendencies toward leadership ability, imaginative capacity, vulnerability to stress, feelings of alienation, and fear of risks seem to be inherited. Conversely, the researchers found that aggression, achievement, orderliness, and social closeness were more related to environmental influences.

45. Social scientists and psychologists refer to the debate of inherited vs. environmental influences as "nature versus nurture." Which of the following sets of twins was most likely influenced by nurture to perform their described behavior?

  (1) Both Jim and John are highly imaginative and enjoy successful careers as political cartoonists.

  (2) Nora and Cora have found that their passion for neatness has paid off in their successful housecleaning business.

  (3) Missy and Cissy were always the ones chosen team captains, club presidents, and office managers.

  (4) Darrell and Dwayne have been loners since childhood and rarely reach out for friendships.

  (5) Both Amy and Anna, equally intelligent, have been hampered in their careers by lack of creativity and daring.

46. Identical twins are created when a single fertilized egg divides to form two offspring of the same biological makeup. Fraternal twins are created when two eggs are fertilized by different sperm, resulting in offspring who are no more alike biologically than any other two siblings. Identical twins raised in separate environments are considered to be ideal subjects for nature vs. nurture studies largely because

  (1) their natural influences are different, but their environmental influences have been the same

  (2) their natural and environmental influences have been the same

  (3) their natural and environmental influences have always been different

  (4) their natural influences are the same, but their environmental influences often are different

  (5) their natural influences are not as easily separated from their environmental influences as is the case for fraternal twins

47. Identical twins raised together share not only their biological identities but also a special intimacy that can be either mysteriously wonderful or strangely destructive. For example, a set of twins in Wales became so attached to each other that they rarely spoke to anyone else and made every move together. After taking part in a minor crime spree, they were sentenced to an institution for the chronically insane. From these facts you can infer that they were placed in an insane asylum because

  (1) their crimes were thought to be especially evil

  (2) their behavior was deemed extremely dangerous to society

  (3) their mental instability was considered to be the reason for their behavior

  (4) their special intimacy was ruled to be the reason for their crimes

  (5) their status as twins would have caused too much fuss in a regular prison setting

ANSWERS ARE ON PAGE 84.

Geography

Text pages
211–231

Questions 1–3 are based on the map below.

LAND USE, NORTH AMERICA

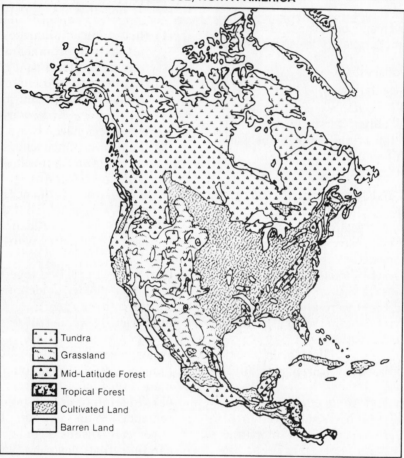

Tundra
Grassland
Mid-Latitude Forest
Tropical Forest
Cultivated Land
Barren Land

1. Which of the following statements is adequately supported by information given on the map above?

   (1) Several different types of crops can be grown in Alaska.
   (2) Canada has much fertile farmland.
   (3) Central America has almost no tillable land.
   (4) The western United States has relatively little cropland.
   (5) Mexico is plagued with great expanses of barren land.

2. Tundra land is found only in the

   (1) far north frigid areas
   (2) western mountain ranges
   (3) central plains
   (4) warm southern regions
   (5) eastern coastlines

3. Lumbering industries are most likely to prosper in

   (1) northern Canada
   (2) the midwestern United States
   (3) central Mexico
   (4) the Eastern seaboard of the United States
   (5) Alaska's northwest

36

ANSWERS ARE ON PAGE 84.

Questions 4–7 are based on the following passage.

Americans are a mobile people, moving often in search of the perfect job, climate, or environment. To capitalize on this tendency toward wanderlust, publishers have printed guides to help in the elusive quest for the perfect place to live. One such manual lists the following criteria for "the best towns in America":

- a population between 25,000 and 100,000
- a location at least fifty miles from any large population area
- moderate local taxes
- local regulations that guide land-use planning and protect environmental health
- no proximity to any known human-made or natural hazards

4. One city's exclusion from the select group of best towns because of its location near a nuclear power plant violates the criterion of

(1) population between 25,000 and 100,000
(2) location at least fifty miles from any large population area
(3) moderate local taxes
(4) local regulations that guide land-use planning and protect environmental health
(5) no proximity to any human-made or natural hazards

5. A town in the state of Washington that prohibits burning of leaves within its borders would win points because it would meet the criterion of

(1) population between 25,000 and 100,000
(2) location at least fifty miles from any large population area
(3) moderate local taxes
(4) local regulations that guide land-use planning and protect environmental health
(5) no proximity to any human-made or natural hazards

6. A midwestern town of 30,000 has reduced its taxes below the national average of $600 and recently passed zoning laws to ensure that it retains its pleasant atmosphere. Its location 75 miles from Kansas City, the closest metropolitan area, puts it in the middle of a tornado zone. It fulfills all criteria of best town *except*

(1) population between 25,000 and 100,000
(2) location at least fifty miles from any large population area
(3) moderate local taxes
(4) local regulations that guide land-use planning and protect environmental health
(5) no proximity to any human-made or natural hazard

7. Of the five criteria listed, the *least* objective criterion is

(1) population between 25,000 and 100,000
(2) location at least fifty miles from any large population area
(3) moderate local taxes
(4) local regulations that guide land-use planning and protect environmental health
(5) no proximity to any known human-made or natural hazards

ANSWERS ARE ON PAGES 84–85.

Questions 8–12 are based on the following graph.

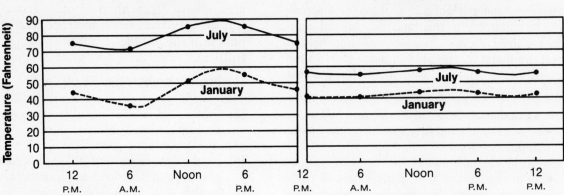

INTERIOR CLIMATE
El Paso, Texas

WINDWARD COASTAL CLIMATE
North Head, Washington

8. The yearly temperature range (difference between highest and lowest temperatures) of El Paso, Texas, is

   (1) over 50 degrees
   (2) about 30 degrees
   (3) about 20 degrees
   (4) about 15 degrees
   (5) under 10 degrees

9. What part of the day tends to be warmest in El Paso?

   (1) early morning
   (2) midmorning
   (3) about noon
   (4) midafternoon
   (5) early evening

10. Interior climates are defined as continental; windward coastal climates as marine. Which of the following statements is adequately supported by information given in the graphs above?

   (1) Continental climates are cooler than marine climates throughout the year.
   (2) Marine climates are cooler than continental climates throughout the year.
   (3) Continental climates have more variety in temperature than do marine climates.
   (4) Marine climates have more variety in temperature than do continental climates.
   (5) Continental and marine climates are very similar in temperature.

11. On a line graph, a bell-shaped curve represents a normal distribution. The curve shows the range one would expect as normal when a number of temperatures are plotted on a graph. Of the two cities shown, El Paso's temperatures are closest to a bell-shaped pattern. This fact supports the conclusion that

   A. North Head's temperature distribution is not considered normal compared to that of most U.S. cities
   B. El Paso's average temperatures in January and July are abnormal
   C. El Paso's average temperatures in January and July are likely to be more similar to other U.S. cities than North Head's are

   (1) A
   (2) B
   (3) C
   (4) A and B
   (5) A and C

12. Which of the following cities is likely to have temperatures most like North Head's?

   (1) Phoenix
   (2) Minneapolis
   (3) Detroit
   (4) San Francisco
   (5) Honolulu

ANSWERS ARE ON PAGE 85.

Questions 13–15 are based on the following terms.

Arctic Zone—the north polar region of the Earth known for its extremely cold temperatures and lack of sunshine

North Temperate Zone—the region of the Earth north of the Equator characterized by moderate temperatures and a change of seasons

Torrid Zone—the region of the Earth north and south of the Equator characterized by intense heat and frequent rain

South Temperate Zone—the region of the Earth south of the Equator characterized by moderate temperatures and a change in seasons

Antarctic Zone—the south polar region of the Earth known for extremely cold temperatures and a lack of sunshine

13. Hawaii is 20 degrees north of the Equator, has little noticeable difference in seasons, and is pleasantly warm most of the year. It is one of the southernmost spots in the

    (1) Arctic Zone
    (2) North Temperate Zone
    (3) Torrid Zone
    (4) South Temperate Zone
    (5) Antarctic Zone

14. *Monsoons*, occurring in southern Asia, are heavy rains accompanied by strong winds and no relief from heat. They occur primarily in the

    (1) Arctic Zone
    (2) North Temperate Zone
    (3) Torrid Zone
    (4) South Temperate Zone
    (5) Antarctic Zone

15. Part of Alaska is so cold year round that its land is a vast tundra, or marshy plain, unable to grow anything but lichens, a type of plant requiring little sunlight. This part of the state is in the

    (1) Arctic Zone
    (2) North Temperate Zone
    (3) Torrid Zone
    (4) South Temperate Zone
    (5) Antarctic Zone

Questions 16 and 17 are based on the following diagram.

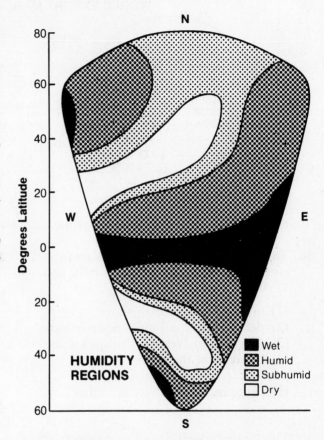

16. This diagram of a hypothetical continent shows a general pattern of predicted humidity. According to the diagram, the largest area of high humidity is at

    (1) the northernmost point of the continent
    (2) the southernmost point of the continent
    (3) about 20 degrees north of the equator
    (4) about 20 degrees south of the equator
    (5) the equatorial region of the continent

17. In general, the west coast of the continent tends to be

    (1) more humid than the east coast
    (2) more arid than the east coast
    (3) as humid as the east coast
    (4) more humid in its northern region than in its southern region
    (5) more arid in its northern region than in its southern region

ANSWERS ARE ON PAGE 85.

Questions 18–22 are based on the following graphs.

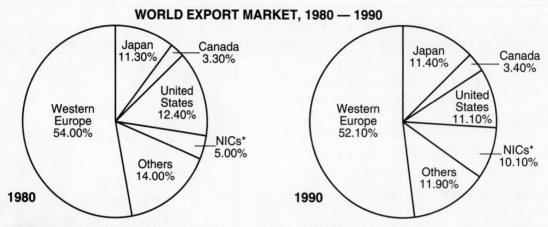

WORLD EXPORT MARKET, 1980 — 1990

*Newly industrialized countries: Brazil, Hong Kong, India, Mexico, Singapore, South Korea, Taiwan, Yugoslavia

18. The biggest change by percentage in the world export market between 1980 and 1990 was the

(1) increase in Canada's share
(2) decrease in the United States' share
(3) decrease in Western Europe's share
(4) increase in the share of newly industrialized countries
(5) decrease in the share of "other" countries

19. The newly industrialized countries (NICs) of Brazil, Hong Kong, India, Mexico, Singapore, South Korea, Taiwan, and Yugoslavia have made a dent in the world export market by becoming low-cost producers of products like raw steel and television sets. This recent surge into the world market has most likely been helped by the

(1) abundance of natural resources in the NICs
(2) high level of education and training in the NICs
(3) low wages the workers of NICs are willing to accept
(4) high rate of inflation worldwide
(5) decreasing cost of oil in the world market

20. According to the graphs, which country suffered a loss in its share of total world exports?

(1) South Korea
(2) Germany
(3) the United States
(4) Japan
(5) Canada

21. These graphs suggest that the country with the largest share of the world export market in 1990 was

(1) Canada
(2) Japan
(3) the United States
(4) South Korea
(5) Taiwan

22. The United States' share in the export market decreased slightly over the ten years shown, but America still led the world in areas such as the manufacturing of semiconductors, personal computers, and jet engines. These facts support the opinion that

(1) the United States has permanently lost its lead in the export of certain products
(2) the United States excels in exporting complex products
(3) the United States could again take the lead in the export of mass-produced goods
(4) the domestic automobile industry has improved because of intense foreign competition
(5) the overinflation of the American dollar caused problems with the United States' trade deficit

ANSWERS ARE ON PAGES 85-86.

Questions 23–29 are based on the following map.

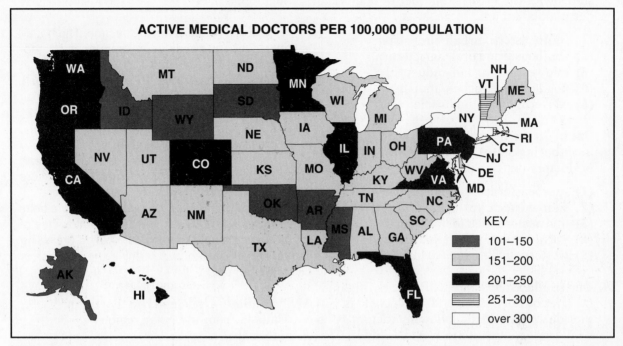

ACTIVE MEDICAL DOCTORS PER 100,000 POPULATION

KEY
- 101–150
- 151–200
- 201–250
- 251–300
- over 300

23. According to the map, in 1990 the ratio of doctors to people in Alaska was

(1) 101–150 per 100,000 people
(2) 151–200 per 100,000 people
(3) 201–250 per 100,000 people
(4) 251–300 per 100,000 people
(5) over 300 per 100,000 people

24. *Demographics* are statistics that describe a population. The demographics of a country give us measurable facts by which we can judge its standard of living. The ratio of doctors to patients is one measure of standard of living—the more doctors, the higher the standard. Which of the following states had the lowest standard of living in 1990, according to this measure?

(1) Alabama
(2) South Dakota
(3) New York
(4) Maine
(5) Pennsylvania

25. Mississippi's population is more than four times that of Washington D.C.; however, the District of Columbia has a ratio of 615 doctors per 100,000 people while Mississippi's is 133 per 100,000. Which of the following is the *best* explanation for Washington's high ratio of doctors to people?

(1) Washington, D.C., is urban, densely populated, and wealthy; Mississippi is rural, sparsely populated, and poor.
(2) Mississippi's citizens tend to avoid seeking medical treatment more than most Americans.
(3) Washington's stressful environment requires more doctors than Mississippi's stress-free environment.
(4) Malpractice insurance premiums cost more in Mississippi than in Washington, D.C.
(5) More hospitals exist in Washington, D.C., than in the entire state of Mississippi.

26. Which of the following demographic characteristics does *not* affect the number of doctors per 100,000 people?

(1) location of the state
(2) wealth of the population
(3) character of the economy
(4) population density
(5) total land area of the state

ANSWERS ARE ON PAGE 86.

27. Based on the information in the map, the states with the *greatest* number of doctors per population tend to be

(1) southeastern, urban, industrial
(2) southeastern, rural, agricultural
(3) midwestern, urban, industrial
(4) northeastern, urban, industrial
(5) western, urban, industrial

28. Based on the information in the map, neighboring states with the *fewest* number of doctors per population tend to be

(1) southeastern, urban, industrial
(2) southeastern, rural, agricultural
(3) midwestern, urban, industrial
(4) northeastern, urban, industrial
(5) western, urban, industrial

29. One southeastern state with a fairly high number of doctors per 100,000 people is Florida. Which of the following factors would *not* contribute to Florida's higher ratio of doctors to people?

(1) It is more urban than its neighbors.
(2) Its citizens are wealthier.
(3) It is home to a growing number of industries.
(4) It has a better climate than its neighbors.
(5) It has become the most populous southeastern state.

---

30. According to current statistics based on the number of practicing physicians and the projected number of medical school graduates, the United States will experience a glut of doctors over the coming decades. From this fact you can infer that

(1) more doctors will continue to specialize
(2) hospital costs will skyrocket
(3) doctors will be forced to retire earlier than before
(4) salaries for doctors will decline dramatically
(5) hospitals will be run increasingly like big businesses

Questions 31 and 32 are based on the following passage.

Equatorial Africa is hot all the time. The hot air is lightweight and has little pressure on it, so geographers say that this area of Africa and other spots near the equator are in a *low-pressure belt*. The Arctic and Antarctic are always cold. Cold air is very heavy and so creates *high pressure belts*.

As patches of highs or lows move from the main pressure belts, the weather is affected. Air from the high-pressure belts brings relatively clear, calm, cool weather with it; whereas low-pressure patches cause stormy, cloudy, warm weather.

The movement of air from these pressure belts generates wind. Dominant winds that follow one of the patterns described above are called prevailing winds. Prevailing winds determine the weather or climate of an area.

31. Prevailing winds entering northern Canada from the polar regions would generally bring

(1) heavy, cloudy weather
(2) warm, clear weather
(3) clear, cool, calm weather
(4) stormy, cloudy weather
(5) cold, stormy weather

32. Prevailing winds entering the Midwest from the Gulf of Mexico would generally bring

(1) heavy, cloudy weather
(2) warm, clear weather
(3) stormy, cloudy, warm weather
(4) clear, calm, cool weather
(5) cold, stormy, weather

ANSWERS ARE ON PAGE 86.

Questions 33–36 are based on the following description of types of maps.

topographical—shows geographical land features of an area

population—explains distribution of people within an area

world—depicts the entire world in order to compare facts from all over the globe

weather—describes current or forecasted weather and climate

political—outlines borders between countries, states, or territories; shows trade relationships among countries; and indicates systems of government

33. A map that depicts the movements of the Allied armies in Europe during World War I is a

   (1) topographical map
   (2) population map
   (3) world map
   (4) weather map
   (5) political map

34. Which kind of map would best show the number of minority group members in the city and suburbs of a metropolis?

   (1) topographical map
   (2) population map
   (3) world map
   (4) weather map
   (5) political map

35. A map showing average annual snowfall in a region would be called a

   (1) topographical map
   (2) population map
   (3) world map
   (4) weather map
   (5) political map

36. As part of military training, army recruits are required to pass a test on orienteering. In orienteering, the soldier is given a time limit in which to cover unfamiliar territory by using a map and a compass. The type of map that would be most useful in this task would be a

   (1) topographical map
   (2) population map
   (3) world map
   (4) weather map
   (5) political map

Questions 37 and 38 are based on the passage below.

   The Mississippi Delta extends about two hundred miles in the direction of the Gulf of Mexico. It has taken thousands of years for the Mississippi River to create its delta, a triangular region of rich land formed by the deposit of sediment. The delta is still growing, spreading out toward the Gulf at the rate of about 330 feet a year.

37. At a rate of 330 feet a year, the delta spreads about one mile every

   (1) 8 years
   (2) 16 years
   (3) 100 years
   (4) 10 years
   (5) 50 years

38. Deltas are characteristically fertile, well watered, and nearly level. All these features together would best explain why the world's deltaic regions

   (1) have a characteristic triangular shape
   (2) seldom have drainage problems
   (3) are constantly flooding
   (4) are highly desirable population centers
   (5) are not located on all the world's continents

ANSWERS ARE ON PAGE 86.

Questions 39–42 are based on the following map.

TIME ZONES ACROSS NORTH AMERICA

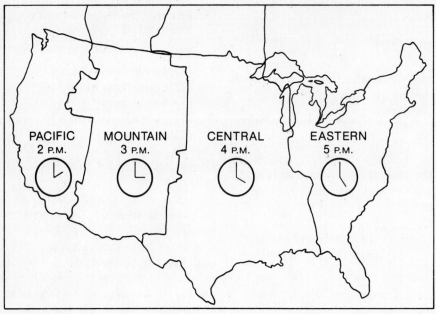

39. New Year's is first celebrated in the United States in

  (1) the Eastern Time Zone
  (2) the Central Time Zone
  (3) the Mountain Time Zone
  (4) the Pacific Time Zone
  (5) all time zones simultaneously

40. According to the map above, what time is it in Denver when it is 1:00 A.M. in Chicago?

  (1) 3:00 A.M.
  (2) 2:00 A.M.
  (3) 11:00 A.M.
  (4) midnight
  (5) noon

41. If you wanted to call a business that closed at 5 P.M. in Seattle, Washington, by what time would you have to call from Dallas, Texas?

  (1) 2:00 P.M.
  (2) 3:00 P.M.
  (3) 4:00 P.M.
  (4) 5:00 P.M.
  (5) 7:00 P.M.

42. The only time of the year when northwestern Indiana and the rest of the state are on the same schedule is during the spring and summer when daylight saving time (DST) is in effect. During daylight saving time clocks are set ahead one hour so that daylight lasts longer. Which of the following is *not* a logical conclusion that you can draw from the facts provided?

  (1) Most of Indiana remains on standard time the year round.
  (2) In Indiana, only the northwestern part of the state observes DST.
  (3) All fifty states are not required by law to observe DST.
  (4) Indiana is the only state that is exempt from observing DST.
  (5) Northwest Indiana does not fall within the same time zone as the rest of the state.

ANSWERS ARE ON PAGE 87.

Questions 43 and 44 are based on the following passage.

Nearly 75 percent of the world's surface is water, yet it is the most critically short of all the natural resources. It is vital to human survival, each one of us requiring at least two or three quarts per day. Some of us, however, use more than fifty gallons a day. The misuse and overuse of water in some parts of the world, the difficulty in transporting the resource from water-rich areas to arid spots, and the pollution of many fresh water sources have all contributed to the irreversible shortage.

43. Which of the following statements is an opinion expressed or implied in the passage above?

(1) Nearly 75 percent of the world's surface is water.

(2) A severe water shortage exists in the world.

(3) One person's use of fifty gallons of water per day constitutes misuse.

(4) Much difficulty is encountered in transporting water across great distances.

(5) The pollution of many fresh water sources has contributed to the shortage.

44. A paradox is a statement that is seemingly contradictory or opposed to common sense yet is true. The paradox evident in the passage above is that

(1) people misuse and waste water

(2) most of the Earth's surface is water but a shortage exists

(3) people can live off less than three quarts of water per day

(4) many fresh water sources are polluted

(5) water is difficult to transport

45. In which region of the United States is water used for human consumption the most plentiful?

(1) the Pacific Northwest

(2) the Northeast

(3) the Southwest

(4) the Middle Atlantic

(5) the North Central

ANSWERS ARE ON PAGE 87.

Economics

Text pages
233–255

Questions 1–4 are based on the following terms.

pure capitalism—an economic system based on the private ownership of property and freedom of choice for consumers, with little or no governmental intervention

authoritarian socialism—an economic and social system in which private property is not permitted and the government subordinates individual choice to state-determined goals

liberal socialism—an economic system under which a country's major industries and services are owned both publicly and cooperatively, and some governmental planning determines goals

manorial feudalism—an economic and social system in which one class of people provides protection and shelter for a lower class that pledges it loyalty and service

mercantilism—an economic system advocating commercial dominance over other nations, a buildup of gold reserves, a favorable balance of trade, and agricultural and industrial development

1. The economies of communist Vietnam, North Korea, and Cuba, in which goods are owned in common and private property is eliminated, are based on a system most similar to

   (1) pure capitalism
   (2) authoritarian socialism
   (3) liberal socialism
   (4) manorial feudalism
   (5) mercantilism

2. The practice of imposing tariffs on imported goods in order to encourage the purchase of domestically manufactured goods originated under the economic system of

   (1) pure capitalism
   (2) authoritarian socialism
   (3) liberal socialism
   (4) manorial feudalism
   (5) mercantilism

3. A laissez-faire economy is characterized by competition among producers without governmental intervention. Another name for this economic system is

   (1) pure capitalism
   (2) authoritarian socialism
   (3) liberal socialism
   (4) manorial feudalism
   (5) mercantilism

4. In the sharecropping system of the South, tenant farmers are provided credit for seed, tools, and living quarters. They work the owner's land and agree to share the crop's value with the owner. This system is similar to

   (1) pure capitalism
   (2) authoritarian socialism
   (3) liberal socialism
   (4) manorial feudalism
   (5) mercantilism

5. During times of rapid inflation, loss of real income can occur if wages do not increase at the same rate as prices. Which of the following is a popular demand made by labor unions to correct this imbalance?

   (1) good medical and education benefits
   (2) shorter work weeks
   (3) seniority rights during lay-offs
   (4) cost-of-living adjustments
   (5) automatic predetermined raises

6. A major feature of a recession or a depression is high unemployment. A typical indicator of a healthy GNP (gross national product) is high employment. Therefore, we can conclude that during a recession or depression the GNP would

   (1) be low
   (2) be high
   (3) fluctuate
   (4) be unaffected
   (5) be wiped out

ANSWERS ARE ON PAGE 87.

Questions 7–10 are based on the following graph.

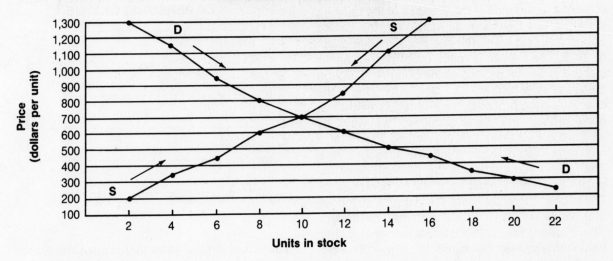

SUPPLY AND DEMAND OF VCR'S AT VIC'S ELECTRONICS STORE

Equilibrium is described as the point at which the supply of a product equals the demand for it, establishing the market price. When the price is greater than the equilibrium point, demand falls and a surplus occurs. When the price falls below the equilibrium point, demand increases and a shortage occurs.

7. What is the market price for VCRs at Vic's Electronics?

   (1) $300
   (2) $600
   (3) $700
   (4) $900
   (5) $1,000

8. What is the ideal number of VCRs that Vic's can stock that would result in neither a surplus nor a shortage?

   (1) 2
   (2) 4
   (3) 6
   (4) 8
   (5) 10

9. At what price did Vic's Electronics find they could sell two more VCRs than they normally had a demand for?

   (1) $300
   (2) $600
   (3) $700
   (4) $900
   (5) $1,000

10. Which of the following statements can be adequately supported by the information given in the graph?

    (1) If Vic's Electronics offered extended warranties on its VCRs, then the units would sell better.
    (2) If Vic's Electronics put its higher-priced VCRs on sale, it could sell them faster.
    (3) If Vic's Electronics remodeled its store, it would attract more customers and sell more VCRs.
    (4) If Vic's Electronics advertised more, it could create more demand for its higher priced VCRs.
    (5) Vic's Electronics stocked larger numbers of higher priced VCRs than it could sell.

ANSWERS ARE ON PAGE 88.

Questions 11 and 12 are based on the following passage.

The Federal Reserve System was created to prevent a recurrence of the collapse of the banking system and subsequent depression in the United States that occurred after the stock market crash of 1929. The system is made up of district banks located in twelve regions of the country. Through these banks (which are also clearinghouses in the check-clearing process), the Fed regulates the nation's money and credit supplies. Two ways by which the Fed does this are setting the reserve requirement and determining the discount rate. The *reserve requirement* is the percentage of deposits that banks must earmark as nonlendable. Therefore, it directly limits the amount of money that banks are allowed to lend to their customers. The *discount rate* is the interest rate that district banks charge member banks to borrow. The discount rate indirectly sets the interest rate that consumers will pay for their loans.

11. What action would the Fed take if it wanted to decrease the money supply during a period of inflation?

    (1) demand that the banks hold less money in reserve
    (2) demand that the banks hold more money in reserve
    (3) decrease the discount rate to the banks
    (4) decrease the commercial loan rate to the public
    (5) determine what reserve ratio and discount rate the banks wanted

12. If the Federal Reserve System were to charge its member banks a discount rate of 10 percent, which of the following would be the most likely rate charged on commercial loans?

    (1) 4 percent
    (2) 6 percent
    (3) 8 percent
    (4) 10 percent
    (5) 12 percent

Question 13 is based on the following graph.

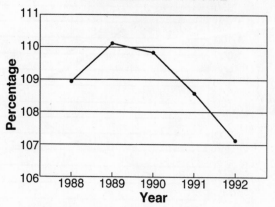

INDIVIDUAL DEBT AS A PERCENTAGE OF PERSONAL INCOME

13. Based on the information in this graph, what was the relationship between individual debt and personal income during the five-year period shown?

    (1) Individual debt exceeded personal income.
    (2) Individual debt increased in proportion to personal income.
    (3) Individual debt and personal income held steady throughout.
    (4) Individual debt and personal income fluctuated together.
    (5) Individual debt forced a lowering of personal income.

ANSWERS ARE ON PAGE 88.

Questions 14–16 are based on the following chart.

"Do you favor or oppose the following specific approaches to cutting the deficit?"

	FAVOR	OPPOSE
A 2 percent increase in federal income-tax rates	32%	63%
A 10 cent-per-gallon gasoline tax	20%	77%
A 2 percent reduction in automatic cost-of-living increases in social security and other benefit programs	27%	69%
An actual decrease in social security benefits for recipients who earn more than $25,000 a year from other sources	55%	40%

---

14. During the 1980s and 1990s deficit spending (the government's practice of spending more than it takes in) reached critical levels. Many solutions were proposed and debated. When responding to these solutions in the poll cited above, to what did people react most positively?

    (1) a 2 percent increase in federal income tax rates
    (2) a 10 cent-per-gallon gasoline tax
    (3) a 2 percent reduction in automatic increases in certain benefit programs
    (4) an actual decrease in social security benefits for those already earning $25,000 or more a year
    (5) a combination of the first three listed

15. A representative to Congress who was sensitive to the wishes of the people would most likely *not* vote for

    (1) a 2 percent increase in federal income tax rates
    (2) a 10 cent-per-gallon gasoline tax
    (3) a 2 percent reduction in automatic increases in certain benefit programs
    (4) an actual decrease in social security benefits for those already earning $25,000 or more a year
    (5) any of the choices listed

16. The information given in the chart supports the statement that the public

    (1) does not want the deficit to be eliminated through higher taxes
    (2) does not want the deficit to be eliminated through reduction in social welfare programs
    (3) would rather be taxed at a higher rate than live in a country with a high deficit
    (4) would rather sacrifice social welfare programs than live in a country with a high deficit
    (5) would favor any proposal that might eliminate or reduce the deficit

---

17. In their first year on the market in Japan, DAT (digital audiotape) recorders received much positive publicity, but they did not sell well. The surprisingly low success of a much-heralded technological improvement can best be explained by the

    (1) trade imbalance between Japan and the United States
    (2) high inflation rate in effect in Japan at the time
    (3) lowering of prices on the machines and their tapes
    (4) small number of prerecorded tapes on the market to use with them
    (5) large number of DAT recorders flooding the market

18. The sluggish sales of Japan's DATs is most similar to which of the following situations that occurred in the consumer electronics industry?

    (1) Japan's domination of the consumer electronics industry
    (2) the entrance of Korean manufacturers into the industry
    (3) the phasing out of Sony's beta-formatted videocassette recorder
    (4) the popularity of VHS-compatible VCRs
    (5) the imposition of quotas on all Japanese imports to the United States

ANSWERS ARE ON PAGE 88.

Questions 19–21 are based on the following definitions of types of unemployment.

cyclical unemployment—unemployment caused by recession or other unstable economic times

structural unemployment—unemployment caused by a rapid change in the character of the economy

frictional unemployment—unemployment caused by workers quitting jobs for reasons of dissatisfaction

seasonal unemployment—unemployment caused by a change from one season or time period to another

"hard-core" unemployment—unemployment that has become ingrained after several generations in a family or community experience joblessness

19. Clinton complained that his job was characterized by a "feast or famine" tendency in which periods of intense activity alternated with periods of absolute idleness. When he quit, his joblessness was described as

    (1) cyclical unemployment
    (2) structural unemployment
    (3) frictional unemployment
    (4) seasonal unemployment
    (5) hard-core unemployment

20. The U.S. economy has become more service-oriented than manufacturing-oriented in recent years. As a result, the country has experienced wide-ranging

    (1) cyclical unemployment
    (2) structural unemployment
    (3) frictional unemployment
    (4) seasonal unemployment
    (5) hard-core unemployment

21. Some sociologists have observed that in many inner-city neighborhoods across the United States, dependence on welfare has become a way of life as children see their parents, grandparents, friends, and neighbors without jobs. These sociologists suggest that training such people would be very difficult and refer to the problem as

    (1) cyclical unemployment
    (2) structural unemployment
    (3) frictional unemployment
    (4) seasonal unemployment
    (5) hard-core unemployment

Questions 22 and 23 are based on the following passage.

How would you like it if the United States government suddenly declared itself bankrupt? No longer would it make good on all those Treasury bills and Treasury bonds you, your neighbors, your parents, your banks, your insurance company, your pension fund, your school system, and your employer have bought.

You want to start a depression real fast? Cause a worldwide crash? This would do it. No more jobs for anybody.

A default by the most powerful economy on the face of the earth would wipe out fortunes and destroy income instantly. The dollar would drop so low that even Zaire wouldn't buy it.

Churches wouldn't even accept it in the collection plate.

22. "The most powerful economy on the face of the Earth" referred to in the passage is

    (1) Zaire
    (2) the United States
    (3) churches
    (4) the Treasury Department
    (5) the banking system

23. From the facts presented in the passage, you can infer that Zaire is

    (1) the poorest nation on the face of the Earth
    (2) the wealthiest nation in Africa
    (3) a Third World nation plagued by poverty and underdevelopment
    (4) the one nation where the dollar's value is most respected
    (5) a nation that is always seeking handouts

ANSWERS ARE ON PAGE 88.

Questions 24–26 are based on the following passage.

The economic growth of a country is measured by the amount of goods and services it produces over a given period of time. The degree of growth depends on a certain combination of characteristics. For optimum growth these characteristics would include:

- an abundance of high quality natural resources
- natural and human-made resources used to full capacity
- the ability and willingness to invest in capital goods
- a labor force capable of growing in size and quality
- a constant increase in aggregate demand (total spending)

24. Large corporations that do not use computers purchased to increase efficiency in production are hurting their economic growth. Which of the following attributes is neglected in this situation?

(1) an abundance of natural resources
(2) full use of available resources
(3) investment in capital goods
(4) a growing, trainable labor force
(5) an increase in aggregate demand

25. A community college gives intensive training to its industrial arts faculty in the latest technology so they can retrain local workers displaced from their jobs. The college is contributing to which factor in economic growth?

(1) an abundance of natural resources
(2) full use of available resources
(3) investment in capital goods
(4) a growing, trainable labor force
(5) an increase in aggregate demand

26. During a recession consumers usually spend less money, putting off purchases until better economic times return. This behavior directly affects which factor related to economic growth?

(1) an abundance of natural resources
(2) full use of resources
(3) investment in capital goods
(4) a growing trainable labor force
(5) an increase in aggregate demand

Questions 27–29 are based on the following terms.

sole proprietorship—a business owned and managed by one person

partnership—an agreement between two or more persons to own and operate a business together

limited partnership—a partnership in which liability for business debts is limited to the amount of money each partner has invested in the business

corporation—a business organization recognized by law to act as a legal person with rights and privileges and whose individual owners are not personally liable for its debts

cooperative—a business enterprise whose owners are its own customers and whose purpose is usually to save money on purchases

27. A group of neighbors and friends who get together to form a business to buy grocery products at wholesale prices may be described as a

(1) sole proprietorship
(2) partnership
(3) limited partnership
(4) corporation
(5) cooperative

28. For which type of business does an owner have unlimited personal liability for all business debts?

(1) sole proprietorship
(2) partnership
(3) limited partnership
(4) corporation
(5) cooperative

29. One similarity between a limited partnership and a corporation is that the owners

(1) are treated as customers in the business
(2) share equally in business decisions
(3) share equally in the business's profits
(4) have limited or no liability for business debts
(5) have personal liability for business debts

ANSWERS ARE ON PAGES 88-89.

Questions 30–33 are based on the following cartoon.

30. The main point of this cartoon is that

(1) the U.S. Congress's tax policies are detrimental to the economy
(2) economic growth is preventing Congress from eliminating the deficit
(3) fast-rising taxes can help increase economic growth
(4) taxes can be eliminated only at the expense of economic growth
(5) representatives in Congress are the driving force behind economic growth

31. The cartoonist makes the judgment that congressional tax policy

(1) is frightening the country
(2) is wrong; the direction of the economy is right
(3) is right; the direction of the economy is wrong
(4) will reduce the deficit
(5) will result in a showdown with the president

32. Based on the information in the cartoon and the general effect on economic growth, you can conclude that when this cartoon was drawn, Congress was recommending

(1) a decrease in taxes to keep economic growth going

(2) an increase in government spending to fuel the economy
(3) maintaining the existing level of taxes
(4) an increase in taxes to fund federal programs or reduce the budget
(5) a decrease in government spending to dampen economic growth

33. Several years after this cartoon was published, Congress passed a bill designed to cut the federal budget deficit. The bill raised income taxes on wealthy Americans, Medicare taxes, gasoline taxes, and taxes on Social Security benefits. If this cartoon is an accurate reflection of the cartoonist's economic and political views, you can infer that the cartoonist believed this new law would

(1) encourage economic growth by reducing the federal budget deficit
(2) have little effect on the economy because it only taxed the wealthy
(3) conserve energy by discouraging people from using their cars
(4) reduce national income, and tax income from it, by slowing economic growth
(5) stimulate the economy by encouraging people to work past retirement age

ANSWERS ARE ON PAGE 89.

Questions 34–35 are based on the following graph.

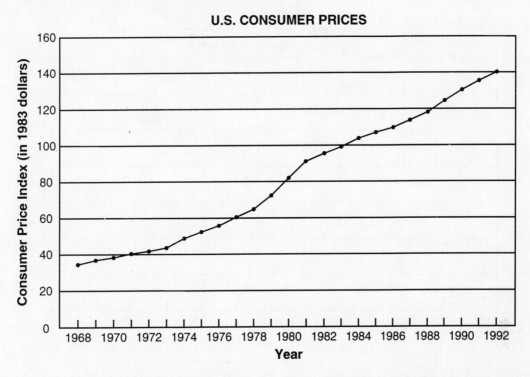

U.S. CONSUMER PRICES

34. Between August 1971 and April 1974, the federal government attempted to control a fast-rising CPI by instituting a series of programs such as price and wage controls. According to the graph, these programs

(1) managed to reverse inflation
(2) helped hold prices steady
(3) were ineffective
(4) had a long-lasting effect
(5) reduced economic growth

35. If the CPI continues its general trend into the next decade, consumer prices by the end of the century can be expected to be

(1) distinctly lower than they are now
(2) about the same as they are now
(3) twice as high as those of 1968
(4) almost 80% higher than those of 1983
(5) ten times greater than those of 1968

36. This CPI is a gauge for measuring a rise in prices, or *inflation*, from year to year by using 1983 prices as a standard. For example, a cordless telephone that cost $100 in 1983 cost $140 in 1992. Based on this definition, the CPI measures an increase in

(1) economic growth
(2) cost of living
(3) supply and demand
(4) balance of trade
(5) gross national product

ANSWERS ARE ON PAGE 89.

Questions 37 and 38 are based on the following graph.

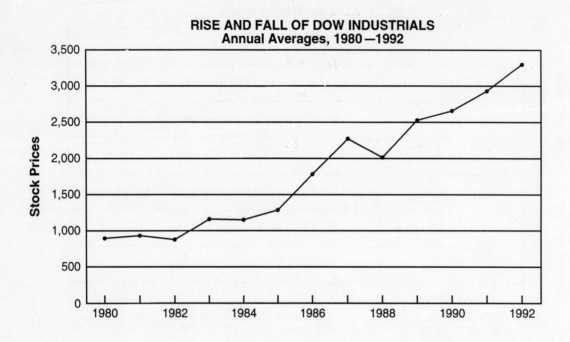

RISE AND FALL OF DOW INDUSTRIALS
Annual Averages, 1980—1992

37. From 1980 to 1985, the Dow industrial average was

(1) fairly stable
(2) steadily falling
(3) rising dramatically
(4) fluctuating up and down constantly
(5) generally rising, but periodically shaky

38. In October 1987 the stock market plunged drastically. One financial expert likened the public reaction he expected to the public response to a disaster such as a plane crash. People are shocked and may be afraid to travel by air for a while, but eventually they do forget their fears and fly again. Did this prediction prove to be accurate?

(1) Yes, the Dow industrial average never recovered from the 1987 crash.
(2) No, the Dow industrial average was never affected by the crash.
(3) Yes, the Dow dropped temporarily after 1987 and then recovered.
(4) No, prices stabilized after the crash.
(5) Yes, prices rose immediately after the crash.

ANSWERS ARE ON PAGE 89.

Questions 39–42 are based on the following chart.

ECONOMIC INDICATORS

	1929	1933	1937	1939	1940	1941	1942	1943	1944	1945
Gross National Product (GNP)	103.4	55.8	90.7	90.8	99.9	124.9	158.3	192.0	210.5	212.3
Personal Income	84.9	46.9	73.8	72.4	77.8	95.3	122.4	150.7	164.4	169.8
Consumer Price Index (CPI) 1967 = 100	51.3	38.8	43.0	41.6	42.0	44.1	48.8	51.8	52.7	53.9
Unemployment (in percent)	3.2	24.9	14.3	17.2	14.6	9.9	4.7	1.9	1.2	1.9

Source: *Economics*, by Campbell R. McConnell, 1978

39. *Economic indicators* are statistics that show economic experts how the economy is performing. These can include the gross national product (GNP), the level of personal income, the consumer price index (CPI), and the unemployment rate in the country. According to the chart, which one of the years listed showed the most severe effects of the Great Depression?

(1) 1929
(2) 1933
(3) 1937
(4) 1939
(5) 1940

40. In 1941, the United States entered World War II. By 1945 the war was nearing an end. Based on the statistics in the chart, America's involvement in the international war

(1) weakened the economy
(2) made the economy healthier
(3) led to a decrease in the GNP
(4) led to a decrease in the CPI
(5) had no measurable effect on the economy

41. Which of the following factors would *best* account for low unemployment during the period 1941 to 1945?

(1) Public work projects such as the CCC (Civilian Conservation Corps) increased the number of available jobs
(2) Factories were at peak production levels as they geared up for the war effort
(3) The Democrats were in charge and created many jobs for the unemployed
(4) Children joined their mothers on the production lines, increasing the number of workers
(5) Relatively few jobs left the country because the foreign labor pool was limited

42. According to the chart, the prices of the 1930s and early 1940s were about

(1) the same as in 1967
(2) half the level of 1967
(3) double the level of 1967
(4) the same as they are now
(5) half the level that they are now

ANSWERS ARE ON PAGE 89.

Questions 43–45 are based on the following passage.

Although nearly 14 percent of the businesses in the United States are corporations, they account for roughly 85 percent of the business transacted. Corporations are owned by stockholders or shareholders who purchase stock or shares in the organization. Stockholders can vote for the corporation's board of directors. One vote is given for each share of common stock owned, so the more stock owned, the more influence wielded.

One advantage of a corporation is that it can raise money for capital investments and improvements by selling bonds as well as by offering additional shares of stock. Bonds are certificates bought by investors that are repaid at a guaranteed rate of interest on a designated maturity date. On the other hand, stockholders earn dividends for the money they invest. Dividends are not guaranteed, however, and are usually paid only when the corporation's profits permit it.

43. One big difference between owning common stock and owning bonds from a corporation is that stockholders

(1) get a guaranteed return on their investment; bond owners do not
(2) get their returns by specified dates each year; bond owners do not
(3) help a corporation financially to improve itself; bond owners do not
(4) vote for the board of directors; bond owners do not
(5) appoint the officers of a corporation; bond owners do not

44. *Preferred stock* is guaranteed priority over common stock in the payment of dividends and in the distribution of assets. If a corporation is forced to dissolve and must pay all its creditors interest and dividends, which would be the proper order in which to pay the claimants?

(1) preferred stockholders, common stockholders, bond owners
(2) common stockholders, preferred stockholders, bond owners
(3) bond owners, common stockholders, preferred stockholders
(4) bond owners, preferred stockholders, common stockholders
(5) common stockholders, bond owners, preferred stockholders

45. The laws for chartering corporations vary from state to state and contain provisions that may protect either the individual private investor or the organizers of the corporation. Most states favor the interests of the individual investor over the organizers (management). A corporation that is chartered in its own state is called a *domestic corporation*. One that is chartered in another state (or nation) is called a *foreign corporation*. The small state of Delaware is home to numerous foreign corporations and is nicknamed the "Corporation State." Based on the facts above, you can infer that Delaware is home to more foreign corporations than any other state because it

(1) does not require corporations to pay taxes at all
(2) has corporation laws more favorable to organizing management's interests than to individual investors' interests
(3) has corporation laws more favorable to individual investors' interests than to management's interests
(4) has laws that favor neither individual investors nor management
(5) actively seeks the business of corporations through advertising campaigns

ANSWERS ARE ON PAGE 90.

Practice Test

Directions: This social studies practice test will give you the opportunity to evaluate your readiness for the actual GED Social Studies Test.

This test contains 60 questions. Some of the questions are based on short reading passages, and some of them require you to interpret a chart, map, graph, or political cartoon.

You should take approximately 85 minutes to complete this test. At the end of 85 minutes, stop and mark your place. Then finish the test. This will give you an idea of whether or not you can finish the real GED Test in the time allotted. Try to answer as many questions as you can. A blank will count as a wrong answer, so make a reasonable guess for questions you are not sure of.

Questions 1 and 2 are based on the following chart.

	Revenue	Income	Earnings	Dividends	Price Range—Common Stock High	Low
	(millions of dollars)		(dollars per share)			
1939	28.0	2.9	4.81	3.00	87¾	55
1940	61.1	10.8	18.05	5.00	94⅞	65⅛
1941	181.4	18.2	30.29	5.00	79¼	59¼
1942	501.8	11.1	15.38	5.00	70¾	51
1943	987.7	6.0	9.92	5.00	72½	47

DOUGLAS AIRCRAFT COMPANY SELECTED STATISTICS, 1939-1943

1. From the facts in the table, you can infer that the single most important factor in the dramatic rise of the aircraft industry during the period shown was the

    (1) beginning of the Great Depression in the United States
    (2) entry of the United States into World War II
    (3) growing strength of labor unions around the world
    (4) increase of leisure time for Americans
    (5) rapid decline of the railroad industry

2. The law of diminishing returns applies when a company's return on investment (profit) does not increase in relation to the additional investment in labor. After what year would this law apply to the Douglas Aircraft Company?

    (1) 1939
    (2) 1940
    (3) 1941
    (4) 1942
    (5) 1943

Questions 3 and 4 are based on the following short passage.

Canada has used the Maple Leaf as a symbol for its flag only since February of 1965. Before that, the country had flown the Red Ensign for 20 years. Though it had replaced the British Union Jack, the Red Ensign still incorporated the Union Jack into its basic design. The Maple Leaf was the first flag of Canada that truly proclaimed its sovereignty from Great Britain.

3. From the context in which it is used, "sovereignty" means

   (1) development
   (2) alliance
   (3) alienation
   (4) patriotism
   (5) independence

4. Which of the following statements is adequately supported by the passage?

   (1) Canada was under the rule of France during the 17th and 18th centuries
   (2) Canada first received a degree of sovereignty from Great Britain in 1867
   (3) Canada's voters did not approve of the Red Ensign
   (4) Canada's ties to Great Britain go back many years
   (5) Canada as a country has never had a history of national pride

5. Separation of church and state as described in the U.S. Constitution is often cited as the reason for prohibiting all of the following *except*

   (1) displaying the Nativity scene on public property
   (2) prayer time in the public schools
   (3) inclusion of religious symbols, such as the cross, on government flags
   (4) election of an ordained minister to public office
   (5) teaching creationism and excluding the theory of evolution in a public school

Questions 6–9 are based on the following passage.

According to the Electronics Industries Association, the United States loses over $9 billion in business and 225,000 jobs every year because of export laws that forbid certain manufacturers to sell militarily sensitive electronic products to foreign countries.

6. Which of the following would benefit *most* from restrictions on the electronics exports described above?

   (1) all foreign concerns that desire to buy American goods
   (2) Japanese exporters who desire a greater share of the American market
   (3) the Commerce Department, which seeks to increase the flow of foreign-made electronics products
   (4) the U.S. auto industry, which has problems similar to the Electronics Industries Association
   (5) the Pentagon, in order to safeguard national security

7. The Electronics Industries Association, which opposes the export ban, apparently places a higher priority on

   (1) jobs for Americans than jobs for foreigners
   (2) its own selfish interests than the interests of others
   (3) profits and jobs for Americans than national security
   (4) national security than jobs for Americans
   (5) trade restrictions than free enterprise

8. In 1993, China allegedly sold missile components to Pakistan. In response, the United States imposed a two-year trade embargo on high-tech sales to China. Which of the following represents the *best* justification for the embargo?

(1) China sold its product to the Pakistanis before selling it to the United States.

(2) U.S. officials had expected China to support American foreign policy in the area.

(3) The missile sale weakened diplomatic relations between the United States and Pakistan.

(4) U.S. security was threatened by the missile sale and by any future sales of weapons developed using high-tech imports.

(5) U.S. military intelligence was not aware that China was selling arms to Pakistan.

9. The facts described above support which group's position regarding restrictions on militarily sensitive exports?

(1) the Electronics Industries Association

(2) Chinese exporters of electronic goods

(3) the U.S. Department of Defense

(4) the U.S. Commerce Department

(5) Chinese consumers of American goods

10. The owners of the Watch Video Store went into business when they found that no other video store existed within a five-mile radius of their location, and many families in the area owned video players. The economic factor that prompted the owners is

(1) supply

(2) demand

(3) surplus

(4) equilibrium

(5) barter

Questions 11 and 12 are based on the following cartoon.

ANOTHER ADDICTIVE ELEMENT THEY DON'T LIKE TO TALK ABOUT...

11. What is the main point the cartoonist is making?

(1) The tobacco industry depends on government subsidies.

(2) Smoking is an unattractive habit.

(3) The tobacco industry has too much power over Congress.

(4) The tobacco industry is weak and vulnerable.

(5) The tobacco industry is dishonest.

12. From the cartoon, you can infer that the tobacco industry

(1) is thriving

(2) is threatened

(3) is also involved in liquor sales

(4) only recently started receiving government aid

(5) has been slow to admit that nicotine is addictive

Questions 13–15 are based on the following passage.

Until Levittown, suburbia was only for the rich and the upper middle class. But Levittown was different. All of its houses were built from the same floor plans; there was no center of town, no industry, no history. Its houses were built explicitly for World War II veterans, and they were affordably priced. They cost $6,990 in 1947, and for this the returning servicemen got a two-bedroom Cape Cod or ranch-style house on a 60-by-100 foot lot and a federally subsidized mortgage of $65 a month. Today the basic, unremodeled version sells for over $125,000 with property taxes of $3,000 to $4,000 a year.

13. The passage suggests that the first Levittowners were

(1) wealthy
(2) upper middle class
(3) middle class
(4) poverty stricken
(5) of all classes

14. The passage cites major drawbacks to living in many suburbs. Which is a disadvantage that is *not* cited?

(1) great distance from the city
(2) no main commercial core
(3) no interesting background
(4) no industrial tax base
(5) fast-rising costs of houses

15. Levittown in 1947 was a highly regulated community. Only carousel-style clothesline dryers were permitted, lawns had to be mowed once a week (or owners were billed for the service), and no blacks were allowed to own or rent houses there. If the Levitts were to set such rules today, they could be punished for violating the

(1) First Amendment of the U.S. Constitution
(2) 1968 Federal Housing Act that forbade racial discrimination in federally financed housing
(3) 1964 Civil Rights Act that outlawed racial discrimination in public accommodations, hiring practices, and voting practices
(4) 1954 Supreme Court decision that racial segregation in public schools is unconstitutional
(5) 1896 Supreme Court decision that approved separate but equal facilities for all races

16. The AARP (American Association for Retired Persons) is the largest special-interest group in the United States and is still growing. Now that one out of nine Americans are dues-paying members and the elderly population is growing more than twice as fast as the rest of the population, certain political issues have come to the forefront. Which of the following would *not* be an issue supported by the Gray Lobby?

(1) Social Security cost-of-living increases
(2) Medicare's paying for prescription drugs
(3) federally-subsidized child day-care centers
(4) government-sponsored nursing home care
(5) government regulations against age discrimination in employment

Questions 17–19 are based on the following cartoon.

17. According to the cartoonist, the values held by "The New American Youth" suggest that they are more

    (1) concerned about the welfare of others than themselves

    (2) understanding about world affairs than adults are

    (3) confident in their abilities than past generations were

    (4) money-oriented than the youth of previous decades were

    (5) rebellious than the youth of other countries

18. The cartoonist probably shares the values of youth who

    (1) have an M.B.A. (Master's of Business Administration)

    (2) are members of the Peace Corps

    (3) are neither young professionals nor members of the Peace Corps

    (4) both seek an M.B.A. degree and are joining the Peace Corps

    (5) reject their parents' values

19. If the cartoonist is correct in his assessment of the values of many of today's youth, one can infer that the number of applicants for the Peace Corps

    (1) is decreasing

    (2) is increasing

    (3) is about the same as in the sixties

    (4) varies according to the state of the economy

    (5) depends on the situation in the world

Questions 20–22 are based on the following passage.

The city of Chicago that was destroyed by the kick of a kerosene lantern on October 8, 1871, was a hustling, bustling hub of industry and transportation, but it was not glamorous. It was dirty and had many unpaved streets and crude wooden structures. After the fire, Chicagoans were determined to reconstruct a more attractive mecca for the immigrants who flocked to it. Laborers of every trade moved to the midwestern city to help in the tremendous task of rebuilding. But in 1873, financial panic and a drop in construction forced huge numbers of workers out of their jobs. Anger and frustration soon developed into riots and bloodshed. Unionism in Chicago was off to a stormy start.

20. According to this passage, unions were started in Chicago because

(1) working conditions were bad
(2) so many people were losing their jobs
(3) there was too much violence in the city
(4) the city had been destroyed by fire
(5) it was no longer an industrial center

21. Which of the following is a stated opinion about Chicago before the fire?

(1) It was an important center for industry.
(2) Many railroads led into and out of it.
(3) It was exciting, but unglamorous.
(4) It had many unpaved streets.
(5) The buildings there were mostly wooden.

22. It can be inferred that the reconstruction of Chicago was done

(1) without proper materials
(2) at too high a cost
(3) by immigrants
(4) by union laborers
(5) within two years

Questions 23 and 24 are based on the following cartoon.

23. What is the main point of this cartoon?

(1) Government claims that the economy is improving are false; the economy is worse.
(2) The rest of the economy may be booming, but the restaurant industry is in a slump.
(3) The new jobs created in America are not going to women.
(4) Recent gains in the economy have not benefitted workers.
(5) American workers complain too much.

24. Which of the following is probably the most important reason the artist uses a waitress as an example in this cartoon?

(1) Many of the new jobs being created are low-paying service positions such as waiting on tables.
(2) He wants to make men more aware of the pressures put on working women.
(3) Waitresses tend to talk more about the economy than other people.
(4) The food industry has been one of the slowest to recover from the recession.
(5) Waitresses are involved in business, so they are in touch with business trends.

Questions 25–28 are based on the following passage.

The Amish have been successful farmers since the 1700s, when they first settled in Pennsylvania in search of religious freedom. They have kept their operations and philosophy simple:

- keep the farm small
- don't take money from the government
- work hard
- help your neighbor
- keep the faith

25. Those who express the opinion that the Amish have prospered because they have not relied on federal subsidies recognize which of the principles of the Amish philosophy?

(1) keep the farm small
(2) don't take money from the government
(3) work hard
(4) help your neighbor
(5) keep the faith

26. The Amish wear plain, dark clothes and depend on the horse and buggy for transportation. This behavior *best* demonstrates the concept of

(1) acculturation
(2) self-actualization
(3) socialization
(4) nonconformism
(5) cultural diffusion

27. Amish children are under tremendous pressure to remain loyal to Amish tradition. Many leave the farm. Those who eventually adopt the behavior of the larger society may be best described as having undergone

(1) socialization
(2) acculturation
(3) cultural diffusion
(4) frustration
(5) self-actualization

28. From the viewpoint of mainstream society, which of the following religious groups might be considered *most* similar to the Amish in terms of being a relatively closed community with its own customs and folkways?

(1) Fundamentalists
(2) Presbyterians
(3) Roman Catholics
(4) Mormons
(5) Lutherans

29. The Federal Reserve Board sets the nation's monetary policy by regulating the supply of money and credit; the president and Congress set fiscal policy by outlining the country's budget, deciding which programs get funding, and considering how the funding will be provided.

Which of the following would be a responsibility of the Federal Reserve Board?

(1) collecting income taxes
(2) limiting defense spending
(3) cutting part of the space program
(4) adding to the transportation budget
(5) setting the reserve requirement for banks

30. The president may exercise the system of checks and balances by

(1) vetoing a bill
(2) overriding the veto of a new bill
(3) rewriting the bill entirely
(4) referring a bill to committees
(5) declaring a bill unconstitutional

31. Congress may exercise the system of checks and balances by

(1) refusing to approve one of the president's cabinet appointments
(2) vetoing a bill proposed by the president
(3) overriding a president's veto of a bill
(4) ruling a law unconstitutional
(5) voting to impeach a president

Questions 32–34 are based on the following passage.

About 80 percent of psychopaths are men, according to some researchers, and these men seem to have brain patterns that are different from most other people's. Neurologically, they do not respond to the threat of danger in the same way as normal people. Emotionally, they are cool and detached, showing no compassion for others or remorse for their actions. Yet behaviorists are reporting success in treating the disorder. These psychologists force the psychopathic patients to confront their hidden feelings of deep despair and to conform to strict rules of behavior. In these cases, psychopaths have actually gained the ability to feel, to learn from experience, and to have hopes and dreams for the future.

32. Which of the following hypothetical patients is a psychopath?

   (1) Tony, who has an unnatural fear of small, closed-in places and will not use elevators, buses, and airplanes
   (2) Judith, who gets depressed very easily and feels anxious most of the time
   (3) Marvin, who feels sick most of the time, but with whom the doctors can find nothing physically wrong
   (4) Kent, who has no long-range goals and who is never sorry for the problems that he causes others
   (5) Corinne, who is so severely disturbed that she often lives in a fantasy world created in her own mind

33. Evidence exists that psychopaths are victims of a nerve disorder. Despite the facts in the passage, it would seem *least* likely that behaviorists would be able to treat psychopaths because behaviorists

   (1) are not medical specialists, and neurologists usually treat nervous disorders
   (2) use only group therapy to treat their patients
   (3) are not recognized by the American Psychological Association
   (4) are not trained criminologists
   (5) are not as effective in their techniques as social workers

34. Many psychopaths are criminals. In one study, 75 percent of those paroled criminals who had been found to be high in psychopathic traits violated their paroles. Twenty percent of those parolees who scored low in psychopathology violated their parole. The only judgment about psychopaths that this information supports is that

   (1) criminals have many psychopathic traits
   (2) psychopathology has a direct connection with all violations of parole
   (3) criminals who violate parole are more likely to be psychopathic than those who do not
   (4) psychopaths have difficulty conforming to rules of behavior
   (5) granting of parole should be prohibited for certain crimes

35. In recent years, France has been experiencing a decline in the birth rate of its native citizens, so it began a national campaign encouraging them to have larger families. The campaign included billboard posters that appealed to their responsibility for ensuring the survival of French culture. Which of the following would likely be *most* effective in stimulating France's population growth?

   (1) ad campaigns that discourage the use of birth control methods
   (2) laws permitting French families to adopt more children
   (3) enacting tax laws favorable to large families of French blood and punitive to small ones
   (4) lowering the age at which couples are permitted to marry
   (5) enacting laws that make it harder to obtain divorces in France

Questions 36–38 are based on the following graph.

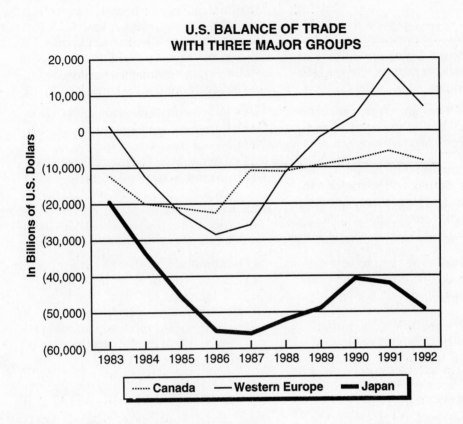

**U.S. BALANCE OF TRADE
WITH THREE MAJOR GROUPS**

...... Canada　——— Western Europe　━━ Japan

36. The U.S. balance of trade with a country is the value of its exports to the country minus the value of its imports from that country. During the period shown on the graph, with which group(s) did the United States have the most *consistent* balance of trade?

(1) Canada
(2) Western Europe
(3) Japan
(4) Japan and Western Europe
(5) Western Europe and Canada

37. Over the years shown, the U.S. balance of trade with Japan

(1) rose slightly
(2) declined steadily
(3) fluctuated, but remained even overall
(4) fluctuated, but declined overall
(5) fluctuated, but eventually rose

38. Which of the following might logically account for the decline in the general U.S. trade balance between 1991 and 1992?

(1) the United States selling more goods abroad
(2) the United States selling fewer goods abroad
(3) the United States depending less on goods imported into the country
(4) the United States depending on a healthy stock market
(5) the United States placing new restrictions on imports

Questions 39–42 are based on the description of the following amendments to the U.S. Constitution.

Fourteenth Amendment—All persons born or naturalized in the United States are citizens of the United States, and no state can deny a U.S. citizen his or her rights.

Fifteenth Amendment—The right to vote cannot be denied any U.S. citizen on the basis of race, color, or previous condition of servitude.

Nineteenth Amendment—The right to vote cannot be denied any U.S. citizen on the basis of sex.

Twenty-Fourth Amendment—The right to vote cannot be denied any U.S. citizen on the basis of failure to pay a poll tax or any other tax.

Twenty-Sixth Amendment—The right to vote cannot be denied any U.S. citizen eighteen years or older on the basis of age.

39. The amendments to the U.S. Constitution are listed in numerical and chronological order. Therefore, it is clear that the right to vote was granted to

    (1) white women before black men or women
    (2) black men before white or black women
    (3) blacks before they were legally declared citizens
    (4) eighteen-year-old males before eighteen-year-old females
    (5) eighteen-year-old whites before eighteen-year-old blacks

40. Many citizens protested state laws requiring a person to be twenty-one or older to be able to vote. After all, some of these citizens who were under the age of twenty-one could be drafted, get married, and enter into certain business transactions. This protest resulted in the

    (1) Fourteenth Amendment
    (2) Fifteenth Amendment
    (3) Nineteenth Amendment
    (4) Twenty-Fourth Amendment
    (5) Twenty-Sixth Amendment

41. One way in which many states circumvented the federal laws requiring them to allow blacks and women to vote was to charge a duty, payable by election day, to anyone wishing to exercise his or her constitutional right. Which of the following amendments outlawed this practice?

    (1) Fourteenth Amendment
    (2) Fifteenth Amendment
    (3) Nineteenth Amendment
    (4) Twenty-Fourth Amendment
    (5) Twenty-Sixth Amendment

42. Charging a tax for the privilege of voting in order to keep certain citizens from voting implies that those citizens

    (1) cannot afford to pay such a tax
    (2) do not fulfill their financial obligations
    (3) would not vote anyway
    (4) are ignorant of constitutional law
    (5) are not full citizens in the eyes of federal law

43. Federalists favored a constitution that provided for a strong central government and uniformity among states. Anti-Federalists were more concerned about the rights of individual citizens and the powers of the state governments. Which of the following aspects of the final draft of the Constitution would the Federalists most likely have approved?

    (1) allowing freedom of religion for individuals
    (2) electing representatives to the House by direct vote of the people
    (3) granting the right to a trial by a jury of peers
    (4) counting three-fifths of the slave population for representation
    (5) disallowing tariffs on goods transported from state to state

Questions 44–46 are based on the following map.

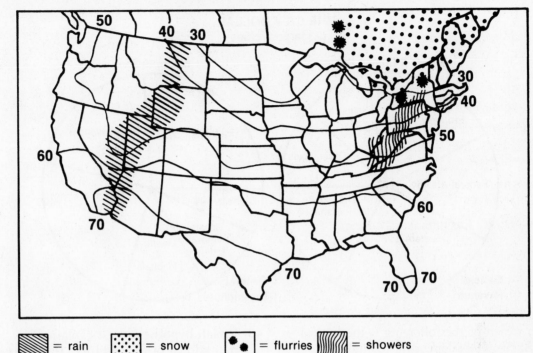

= rain   = snow   = flurries   = showers

44. According to the map above, the temperatures in southern Texas will be most similar to those in

(1) the state of Washington
(2) Illinois
(3) New York
(4) Florida
(5) Oklahoma

45. According to the map, it is unlikely that snow will fall in

(1) Vermont
(2) Maine
(3) New Hampshire
(4) New Mexico
(5) New York

46. Which of the following statements *cannot* be adequately supported by information given on this map?

(1) Generally, temperature patterns cut across the United States horizontally.
(2) Two states are more likely to share weather patterns if they are in the same latitude than if they are in the same longitude.
(3) The United States experiences a broad range of weather patterns in one day.
(4) Some states experience a variety of temperatures and precipitation patterns within their borders.
(5) Precipitation patterns usually start in the west and move across the country in an easterly direction.

Questions 47 and 48 are based on the following graphs.

THE CITY DOLLAR
(23 largest cities)

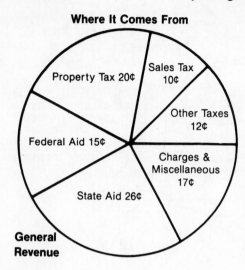

Where It Comes From

Property Tax 20¢
Sales Tax 10¢
Other Taxes 12¢
Federal Aid 15¢
Charges & Miscellaneous 17¢
State Aid 26¢

General Revenue

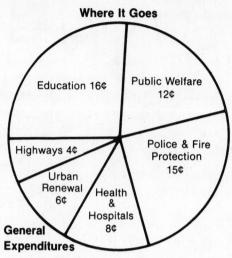

Where It Goes

Education 16¢
Public Welfare 12¢
Highways 4¢
Police & Fire Protection 15¢
Urban Renewal 6¢
Health & Hospitals 8¢

General Expenditures

47. On which of the following is the typical U.S. city *most* dependent for income?

(1) education
(2) property tax
(3) state aid
(4) federal aid
(5) sales tax

48. Which hypothesis best explains the breakdown of expenditures for the twenty-three largest cities represented in the graph?

(1) Urban renewal is of utmost urgency to large U.S. cities.
(2) Cities pay more for highways than states and the federal government do.
(3) Health and hospitals are given a higher priority than public welfare.
(4) The quality of police and fire protection is on the decline in most cities.
(5) Protection and education of their citizens are important functions of most cities.

49. When President Truman declared that "Liberty can be endangered by the 'Right' as well as by the 'Left'," he was referring to the danger of

(1) communist influence in the United States
(2) 'witchhunts' for communist sympathizers in the country
(3) the Korean conflict escalating to full-scale war
(4) states on either coast competing with each other
(5) Democrats and Republicans arguing in Congress

Questions 50–53 are based on the following labels applied to certain groups before, during, and after the Civil War.

abolitionist—one who strongly favored the abolishing of slavery

secessionist—one who favored slave states' breaking away from the Union

confederate—one who joined in the cause of the southern states that seceded from the Union

carpetbagger—a northerner who moved to the South during Reconstruction to take advantage of business and political opportunities

scalawag—a white southerner who supported the efforts of the North in rebuilding the South

50. General P.G.T. Beauregard, a former Confederate officer, supported the Union's efforts to reconcile after a long, bitter, bloody battle. He would have been described by fellow southerners as a(n)

   (1) abolitionist
   (2) secessionist
   (3) confederate
   (4) carpetbagger
   (5) scalawag

51. A northern native who packed only what necessities he could carry and moved to the South after the war in search of get-rich-quick schemes was called a(n)

   (1) abolitionist
   (2) secessionist
   (3) confederate
   (4) carpetbagger
   (5) scalawag

52. One who joined the Underground Railroad before and during the war to help slaves escape to the North or Canada was considered a(n)

   (1) abolitionist
   (2) secessionist
   (3) confederate
   (4) carpetbagger
   (5) scalawag

53. Poor Appalachian whites who feuded with planters and who joined the reconstruction efforts as a way of retaliating against their former southern enemies were called

   (1) abolitionists
   (2) secessionists
   (3) confederates
   (4) carpetbaggers
   (5) scalawags

Question 54 is based on the following passage.

The media call October 19, 1987, "Black Monday." On that day, the stock market nearly collapsed, plunging over 500 points. Many experts blamed it all on a handful of aggressive young investors who devised a computerized scheme that would provide protection against falling prices.

54. According to the passage, many experts think that the cause of Black Monday was

   (1) the media's exploitation of stock market uncertainty
   (2) fighting among the stock market investors
   (3) a strategy pursued by inexperienced speculators
   (4) the refusal by a few investors to share their secrets
   (5) the failure of the computers to predict the crash

Questions 55 and 56 are based on the following chart.

SCHOOL PROFILES City (Number of students in thousands)	Minorities % of students that are black and Hispanic	Dropouts % who enter ninth grade but left before 4 years*	Assaults Number of cases reported last year	Counselors Ratio to high school students
Boston (56)	63%	46%	410	1/313
Chicago (431)	83%	45%	698	1/398
Houston (192)	81%	41%	128**	1/500
Los Angeles (592)	75%	45%	493	1/298
Miami (255)	75%	NA	909	1/420
New York (939)	72%	34%	1,606	1/623
St. Louis (47)	76%	30%	NA	1/390

*Cities compute rate in different ways; figures include students who moved   NA — Not available   **Arrests

55. According to the information in the chart, which city's schools have the most counselors available in proportion to their students?

(1) Boston
(2) Houston
(3) Los Angeles
(4) New York
(5) St. Louis

56. The dropout rates are deceptive because

(1) the figures include students who moved
(2) the percentages are more difficult to interpret than pure numbers
(3) the cities' sizes vary widely from each other
(4) the percentages of minority students vary greatly
(5) the number of counselors per student are so low

Questions 57–60 are based on the following table and passage.

GROSS PRODUCT—1990 (in billions of dollars)	
United States	5,392
Australia	295
Brazil	388
Canada	570
China	302
France	1,191
Germany	1,488
Italy	1,091
India	292
Japan	2,940
Mexico	241
The Netherlands	279
former Soviet Union	1,097
South Korea	240
Spain	491
United Kingdom	980
Illinois	**272**

The **gross domestic product (GDP)** of a nation is the amount of all goods and services it produces in one year. It is computed four times a year in the United States and shows how the economy is performing. The state of Illinois also computes its gross state product (GSP) and publishes the results for its citizens. If Illinois were a nation, in 1990 it would have ranked fifteenth in the world by GDP, just behind the Netherlands. Furthermore, if Illinois's per capita gross domestic product (GDP per person) were stacked up against that of the major industrialized nations, the state would top all of them except Switzerland, Sweden, and Japan.

57. The term "gross state product" means the

(1) total amount of money each citizen of a state produces in the course of a year
(2) total amount of money each citizen of a state earns during the course of a year
(3) amount of goods and services a state would produce if it were a country
(4) amount of goods and services a state produces as compared to other states
(5) total amount of goods and services a state produces in a year

58. The passage implies that in 1990 Illinois's *per capita* gross domestic product was

(1) higher than Switzerland's
(2) higher than the United States's per capita GDP
(3) lower than that of all nations except Japan, Sweden, and Switzerland
(4) lower than that of all nations except the United States
(5) lower than that of any nation, but higher than that of each of the other forty-nine states

59. Which of the following statements is *not* adequately supported by the information in the passage and table?

(1) Illinois's GSP was lower than the United States's GDP.
(2) Illinois's GSP was lower than India's GDP.
(3) Illinois's GSP was lower than Japan's GDP.
(4) Illinois's GSP was higher than either California's or New York's.
(5) Illinois's GSP ranked favorably among the GDPs of major industrial nations.

60. Per capita personal income is another standard by which states are often ranked. Based on this criterion, Connecticut and New Jersey rank among the top in terms of personal wealth. The characteristic(s) shared by both that would *most* directly contribute to their wealth are their

(1) dense populations and urban character
(2) small size and eastern location
(3) closeness to New York City and attractiveness to the city's rich
(4) diversified economies and highly educated work forces
(5) lower proportion of minorities compared to that of other states

PRACTICE TEST ANSWER KEY

Analysis

1. (2) The United States entered World War II in 1941. The need for aircraft carriers contributed to the increases in revenues for the industry for the years 1941 through 1943.

2. (3) In 1941, the company peaked in its income and earnings, and afterwards it no longer earned such high profits despite a bigger increase in revenue.

Comprehension

3. (5) According to the passage, Canada once flew the British flag as its own, indicating that country was under British rule. However, today Canada has its own flag as a sign of its independence. "Sovereignty" means *independence*.

Evaluation

4. (4) The facts that the British Union Jack was Canada's flag and that the Red Ensign incorporated the design support the statement that Canada's historical ties to Great Britain go back many years.

Application

5. (4) Ordained ministers are not forbidden from taking full part in public political life by any U.S. law. All other choices listed have been contested because of the principle of separation of church and state.

Analysis

6. (5) The passage states that the sale of militarily sensitive electronic products to foreign countries is forbidden. The only party listed that is connected directly to the military is the Pentagon.

Evaluation

7. (3) The passage states that the United States loses money and jobs yearly. The only plausible reason for the Electronics Industries Association's opposition to the ban would be that profits and jobs for Americans are adversely affected.

Analysis

8. (4) The Pakistanis could use the missiles against U.S. interests, therefore the missile sale was a threat to U.S. security. China isn't obligated to concern itself with any other problems mentioned, so these problems don't justify an embargo.

Evaluation

9. (3) The situation shows how technology in the wrong hands can threaten U.S. security, as well as how export restrictions can pressure other nations into supporting our interests.

Comprehension

11. (1) The "addictive element" shown in the cartoon is subsidies. The cartoonist suggests that tobacco companies are addicted to subsidies, just as smokers are addicted to cigarettes.

Analysis

12. (5) The caption suggests that there are two addictive elements that tobacco companies don't talk about. The most obvious addictive element in tobacco companies' products is nicotine.

Comprehension

13. (3) The passage states that before Levittown, only the rich and upper middle class could afford houses in suburbia. The houses were built for returning servicemen who would be seeking jobs after the war. It is unlikely that the poverty-stricken would have been potential buyers of the homes.

14. (1) Distance from the city is the only disadvantage of living in the suburbs that is not cited in the passage.

Application

15. (2) Forbidding blacks to buy houses in Levittown would have violated the Housing Act of 1968, which outlawed racial discrimination in federally financed housing. None of the other choices involve discrimination in housing.

Evaluation

16. (3) Of all the choices listed, only the issue of federally subsidized child day-care centers would not be a priority for the elderly.

17. (4) The "new youth" is portrayed wearing a pin-striped suit, holding an M.B.A. (Master's in Business Administration), and desiring a "piece of the action." An earlier generation is portrayed in more modest dress, advocating the Peace Corps.

18. **(2)** The puzzled look on the woman's face contrasted with the opportunistic look on the man's suggests that the cartoonist is sympathetic to and shares the values of the Peace Corps volunteer.

Analysis

19. **(1)** If the cartoonist is correct about the values of today's youth, a logical conclusion is that interest in the Peace Corps is on the decline.

Comprehension

20. **(2)** According to the passage, many laborers moved to Chicago for jobs but lost them when construction fell. Unions were formed when the laborers began to lose their jobs.

Analysis

21. **(3)** The only opinion among the choices is that Chicago was exciting but unglamorous. The other choices are facts that can be proved.

22. **(5)** The passage states that Chicago was destroyed by fire in 1871 and that by 1873 laborers lost their jobs because of a drop in construction. This decrease in construction jobs indicates that Chicago's reconstruction was completed within two years.

23. **(4)** A "booming economy" generally refers to high *business* profits. The waitress admits that business is booming and that there are more jobs. Her comment suggests, however, that higher profits and new jobs aren't helping workers like her.

24. **(1)** Most of the new jobs created in the past decade have been low-paying work serving the public. By depicting a waitress, the cartoonist shows *why* those new jobs aren't necessarily benefitting workers.

Application

25. **(2)** A federal subsidy is money provided by the government to help support farmers. The Amish have refused this type of support.

26. **(4)** By wearing plain, dark clothes and by relying on outmoded means of transportation, the Amish are not conforming to the behavior of modern-day Americans.

27. **(2)** Acculturation is the process of adopting the customs of the larger society. By leaving the farm and becoming like most Americans, Amish children are becoming acculturated.

28. **(4)** Of the choices given, only the Mormons represent a closed community with customs that are perceived to be outside mainstream American culture.

Comprehension

29. **(5)** The Fed sets the reserve requirement for banks (the amount of money they must keep in reserve and not lend out). All other choices are responsibilities of the president and Congress.

30. **(1)** Only the president can veto a bill and thereby prevent Congress from making it a law.

31. **(3)** Congress can exercise the system of checks and balances by overriding a president's veto. Choices (1) and (5) are powers of the Senate alone; choice (2) is not a power of Congress; and choice (4) is a power of the Judiciary.

Application

32. **(4)** Only Kent has the characteristics of a psychopath that are described in the passage: no goals for the future and no regrets for harm caused other people.

Evaluation

33. **(1)** Behaviorists deal with outward, visible responses to stimuli and are not trained in medicine. Despite the passage's statement that behaviorists are reporting success in treating psychopathology, it appears more likely that a medical specialist in the area of nervous disorders would be most qualified. None of the other choices reflects this inconsistency.

Analysis

34. **(4)** The only judgment that the information supports is that, compared to non-psychopaths, psychopaths often cannot conform to rules of behavior. Each of the other choices are either untrue or are overgeneralizations.

35. **(3)** Of the choices listed, only choice (3), enacting tax laws favorable to large families of French blood, is the most effective action that would help stimulate France's native population because French parents would benefit. Choice (1) would not likely be as effective because no personal incentive is involved. Choice (2) does not address France's problem of a

decline in its native population. Choices (4) and (5) have no direct relationship to the number of children a couple produces.

Comprehension

36. **(1)** Of all three trade groups, Canada shows the least variation in the value of its trade balance with the United States. A relatively even line indicates consistency.

37. **(4)** Dollar figures were lower in 1992 than in 1983, so the overall balance declined. Since figures rose between 1987 and 1990, the decline wasn't steady.

38. **(2)** The U.S. balance of trade with all three groups fell. That means that the value of U.S. exports minus imports was lower than in the previous year. Such a drop could only happen if the United States exported fewer goods and/or imported more.

Analysis

39. **(2)** The Fifteenth Amendment precedes the Nineteenth Amendment. Based on this fact, you can conclude that black men were given the right to vote before white and black women were given the right.

Application

40. **(5)** The Twenty-Sixth Amendment gave eighteen-year-olds the right to vote.

41. **(4)** The Twenty-Fourth Amendment prohibited the levying of poll taxes that were created to prevent poor whites and blacks from voting.

Analysis

42. **(1)** Preventing certain classes of people from voting by levying a poll tax presumes that the citizens being denied the vote could not afford to pay the tax. Otherwise, the poll tax requirement would not be an effective barrier to voting.

Application

43. **(5)** If each state could impose its own tariffs on goods transported across state lines, interstate commerce might be hampered. Because they favored legislation that provided for uniformity among states and a sovereign federal government, Federalists would have approved a ban on the imposing of tariffs on goods transported from state to state.

Comprehension

44. **(4)** According to the temperature band on the map, both Florida and Texas will have temperatures in the 60s and 70s. None of the other states shown will have temperatures in the same band.

Analysis

45. **(4)** New Mexico is located in the Southwest, where the temperatures are predicted to be in the 60s and 70s. All of the other states are located in the Northeast, where snow is predicted.

Evaluation

46. **(5)** Precipitation patterns cannot be determined from the map.

47. **(3)** The graph shows that state aid accounts for 26 cents out of every dollar that the city takes in as revenue—more than any other source.

Analysis

48. **(5)** According to the graphs, education and police and fire protection (at 16 and 15 cents per dollar) are the two highest expenditures for these cities.

49. **(2)** Communists and communist sympathizers are considered to be to the left on the political spectrum. Opponents of communism are described as being to the right. A witchhunt means searching out and harassing people suspected to have communist leanings. President Truman warned against those who were so opposed to communism that they violated U.S. citizens' rights to privacy and freedom of speech.

Application

50. **(5)** Beauregard would have been called a scalawag because he supported the efforts of the North to rebuild the South after the war.

51. **(4)** The term "carpetbagger" was applied to Northerners who moved to the South in search of fortunes immediately after the Civil War.

52. **(1)** The Underground Railroad was a movement in which many abolitionists participated.

53. **(5)** Southern whites who had little to gain financially from the Reconstruction, but who still supported it, were called "scalawags."

Comprehension

54. **(3)** According to the passage, money experts blamed the stock market collapse on a handful of aggressive young investors who devised a computerized scheme to protect themselves against falling prices.

55. **(3)** According to the chart, Los Angeles' schools have one counselor for every 298 students—the highest ratio given.

Analysis

56. **(1)** The chart includes students who moved. This practice is deceptive because the students did not drop out, but may have only left one school district for another.

Comprehension

57. **(5)** The gross national product refers to the total amount of goods and services a nation produces. The gross state product is a comparable indicator; therefore, the gross state product refers to the total amount of goods and services a state produces.

Analysis

58. **(2)** The passage states that Illinois's per capita GDP was higher than that of all countries except Switzerland, Sweden, and Japan. Since the United States is included among the countries, you can infer that Illinois's per capita GDP was higher than that of the United States.

Evaluation

59. **(4)** Illinois is the only state for which a GSP is given. Neither California nor New York (both of which are more populous than Illinois and are heavily industrialized) is included. Since this information is incomplete, the statement that Illinois's GSP was higher than California's or New York's is not supported. All of the other choices are supported by the information.

60. **(4)** Connecticut's and New Jersey's diversified economies and highly educated work force are characteristics that would most directly contribute to their wealth. The greater the variety of jobs available, the more people can be put to work. Also, a highly educated and trained population tends to earn more money than one that is not. None of the other characteristics among the choices are adequate in explaining the wealthiness of the two states.

Use the Practice Test Evaluation Chart below to determine the skill and content areas in which you need to do the most review. Circle any items that you got wrong and pay particular attention to areas where you missed half or more of the items. If you need further practice or review, go back to the appropriate pages in *Contemporary's GED Test 2: Social Studies*. These pages are in *italics*.

CONTENT AREA	SKILL AREA				
	Comprehension (25-36)	Application (37-48)	Analysis (49-76)	Evaluation (77-88)	Total Correct
U.S. History (91-143)	3, 20, 54	50, 51 52, 53	8, 21, 22, 23, 24	4, 9	___ /14
Political Science (145-175)	11, 30, 31	5, 15, 40, 41, 43	12, 39, 42	16	___ /12
Behavioral Sciences (177-209)	13, 14, 55	25, 26, 27, 28, 32	19, 34 35, 56	17, 18, 33	___ /15
Geography (211-231)	44		45	46, 60	___ /4
Economics (233-255)	10, 29, 36, 37, 38, 57		1, 2, 6, 48, 49, 58	7, 47, 59	___ /15
Total	___ /16	___ /14	___ /19	___ /11	___ /60

Answer Key

U.S. HISTORY
Comprehension

1. **(5)** The passage says that Governor Gist was determined that the South be an independent nation, possible only by secession. Since South Carolina was the first to secede, it can be assumed that Gist was an instigator.

Evaluation

2. **(1)** The passage states that Gist had devoted his life to politics, his plantation, and the Methodist Church.

3. **(1)** The last sentence of the passage suggests that labor unions have the power to damage the "struggling economy" of a Third World country.

Analysis

4. **(4)** The passage suggests that labor unions in Third World countries like South Korea are working to gain benefits for the workers at the expense of the economy. Choices (1) and (3) are stated in the passage. Choices (2) and (5) are not assumptions that can be made from the passage.

Comprehension

5. **(4)** The summarizing sentence, "It was the first deed of Indian land to English colonists" is a clue that Samoset was an Indian leader.

Evaluation

6. **(3)** The facts that Manhattan Island was. bought for so little and that Samoset believed that land came from the Great Spirit both suggest that Samoset and other Indians did not perceive land in terms of its monetary value.

Application

7. **(2)** In general, Americans believe that everything material has its price; therefore, the purchase of Manhattan Island and the deeding of Pemaquid land demonstrate this belief. None of the other answer choices is supported by the facts stated in the question.

Analysis

8. **(2)** All of the choices except choice (2) contain a reasonable conclusion that follows from a premise. The statement that the Great Spirit provides land is unrelated to the conclusion that land is endless.

Comprehension

9. **(3)** The capitalization of the words "Great Spirit" and the statement that land belongs to no man suggest that "Great Spirit" refers to a Supreme Being.

Analysis

10. **(3)** The response "it's the man who puts money into my pocket that counts" suggests that Democratic presidents improve economic conditions for minorities more than Republican presidents do.

Evaluation

11. **(1)** The statement "money into my pocket that counts" means that the voter places a high value on financial security.

Comprehension

12. **(3)** Florida is outside of the area outlined as the United States in 1783; it was admitted as a state in 1846.

13. **(2)** California is shown within the borders of the territory acquired in the Mexican Cession.

14. **(2)** Following the Louisiana Purchase, greater expanses of territory were annexed. None of the other choices can be supported by information in this map.

15. **(4)** Only option (4) addresses the role of *women* in the war. Women were most visible in Vietnam as healers.

Analysis

16. **(1)** Until recently, the U.S. military never allowed women to participate in combat.

17. **(4)** The one feature that the five laws have in common is that all controlled the kinds of people who could immigrate to the United States.

Application

18. (4) The amendments to the Immigration and Nationality Acts is the only choice that addresses the issue of employment in certain professions.

Evaluation

19. (4) Wilson spoke of America as "the example of peace." Even after the sinking of the Lusitania, an event for which a declaration of war is justified, Wilson refused to retaliate. This indicates that Wilson placed a high value on peace.

Analysis

20. (5) Choices (1) and (3) are facts, not opinions. Choice (2) is not expressed by the writer, and choice (4) is the opposite of the writer's opinion. The last sentence of the passage expresses the opinion that Wilson was wise not to seek revenge.

Application

21. (4) Carter chose not to risk a war that might have resulted from attacking Iran. Choices (1), (2), and (3) are not peaceful initiatives. Choice (5) is unrelated to peace or war.

22. (4) The Vietcong had fewer resources, fewer soldiers, less food, and lower pay than the Americans during the Vietnam War but are considered by historians to have won the war anyway.

Comprehension

23. (4) According to the passage, the Americans defeated Great Britain, which is described as the greatest superpower at that time in history.

Application

24. (1) The Niagara Movement preceded the NAACP and sought an end to discriminatory practices based on race.

25. (2) Both the American Missionary Association and the Peace Corps relied on volunteers who were willing to leave their homes to help others in need.

Analysis

26. (2) The writer states that German Jews, who were professionals such as doctors and lawyers, were different from the ghetto and eastern European Jews.

27. (1) The second sentence suggests that devout Zionists did not assimilate into the German culture.

28. (4) All of the choices except choice (4) are conclusions that can be drawn from the facts. There is no evidence in the passage to support the assumption that the Indians pressured the British to declare The Proclamation of 1763.

Comprehension

29. (5) Both the broad arrow and the figure of 50 percent indicate that South America imported the most slaves from the fifteenth to the nineteenth century.

Evaluation

30. (4) The Caribbean is a relatively small area, yet it imported 43 percent of the slaves during this time. None of the other choices can be proven by information on this map.

Analysis

31. (2) The passage gives repeated examples of the Soviets preceding the Americans in accomplishing their goals.

Evaluation

32. (3) The author implies they were more impressed with the Soviets' speed than with their own country's plans and perseverance.

Analysis

33. (5) The entire passage emphasizes the Soviets' ability to upstage the United States by preceding it in making technological advances. Choice (5) is the only alternative listed that demonstrates this emphasis.

34. (5) Choice (1) is a fact, not an opinion. Choices (2), (3), and (4) are not opinions expressed in the statement. Choice (5) is another way of saying that "Nicaraguan people were struggling to hang on to their lives, their property, and their homes."

35. (5) The statement that Americans of the 1930s were "a more formidable breed" is an opinion that is signaled in the passage by the word "think."

36. (5) The first paragraph states that the depression followed the stock market crash of October 1929. This indicates that the stock market crash was a cause of the depression.

37. (5) The last paragraph contains the sentence "The others I've interviewed wonder as well." This is a clue that someone was surveying people from the Depression years. None of the other choices can be supported by the evidence.

Application

38. **(5)** Of the choices given, only Appalachia is frequently plagued by poverty, scarcity of jobs, and other economic hardships.

Comprehension

39. **(3)** A pigskin is another term for a football. The pigs are labeled "owners" and "players," both of whom are eating from a money-filled trough.

40. **(3)** Both players and owners are eating as much as they can from a trough of money.

Evaluation

41. **(5)** The cartoonist is portraying greed on the parts of the players and owners. A valid conclusion that can be drawn is that both should give in on their demands.

Comprehension

42. **(2)** The passage divides the territory along the eastern seaboard into three distinct regions and explains the colonists' motives in settling in the regions. None of the other choices is supported by the information in the passage.

43. **(4)** Pennsylvania, known as the Quaker State, was founded by Quakers for religious freedom as well as for economic purposes.

Evaluation

44. **(1)** The author introduces the editorial by referring to the "media's intrusion into a politician's personal life for the entertainment value it offers." This statement is critical of the media. None of the other choices are supported by the information in the passage.

Analysis

45. **(2)** The editorial focuses on the sensationalism of media and assumes that selling newspapers and increasing ratings is more important to the media than reporting the facts.

46. **(5)** By stating that "By and large, the American people want most of all to be entertained—not informed," and by referring to sales figures of certain tabloids, the writer is presenting the opinion that the media is only giving the people what they want.

Evaluation

47. **(2)** Choice (2) is the only situation which compares a private citizen's behavior to that of a candidate or a politician in office.

48. **(3)** The editorial makes no claim about the standards of conduct that should be expected of presidents; it focuses only on the media's reporting about politicians' personal lives. Choices (1), (2), (4), and (5) all are either stated or implied in the editorial.

Application

49. **(3)** Russia was interfering with a Latin American country in placing missiles in Cuba, so it was viewed as an unfriendly act toward the United States. Choices (1), (2), and (4) concerned other countries' internal matters, and choice (5) involved the issue of immigration.

Comprehension

50. **(1)** In the Monroe Doctrine the United States declared that it did have a right to extend its authority over the welfare of countries in the Americas.

Application

51. **(3)** Only Theodore Roosevelt's proclamation that the United States would intervene in Latin American affairs if Europeans threatened interference was viewed as unfavorable by Latin American governments, since such interference violates the right of self-determination. Choice (1) does not mention Latin America specifically.

Analysis

52. **(3)** The situation in Mexico had no effect on the outcome of the Civil War.

Application

53. **(2)** The policy of international corporations hiring cheap foreign labor demonstrates the ideas of domestic jobs being lost and foreign workers being exploited.

Evaluation

54. **(3)** The pastoral statement represented a sensitivity toward the needs of the unemployed and the exploited worker; therefore, you could conclude that

American Catholic bishops supported the value of economic fairness over private profit.

Application

55. (1) Only Choice (1) demonstrates a foreign investor (Union Carbide), attracted by low wages to an undeveloped country (India), exporting jobs and exploiting workers.

Evaluation

56. (1) The descriptive terms "smoking entrails," "carcass of the steer," and "steaming hot blood" suggest that Jurgis works in a slaughterhouse.

Analysis

57. (4) The excerpt states that Jurgis's "whole soul was dancing with joy—he was at work at last. . . ." This supports the statement that he had been unemployed for a long time.

58. (1) The low wages (17½ cents an hour) suggest that the story took place in a very early period. The date 1905 is the only one listed to which this might apply.

Application

59. (2) A policy of laissez faire in government prohibits the interference of government in business practices. Each of the reform acts and laws represented greater involvement of the federal government in business.

60. (3) The Pure Food and Drug Act sets the standards for the production of food and drugs.

61. (4) Only the Child Labor Laws would have jurisdiction over the employment of those under age fifteen.

Evaluation

62. (4) The state's plan could be seen as endorsing one particular religion. The statue did not limit privacy, speech, worship, or the freedom of Baptists.

POLITICAL SCIENCE
Comprehension

1. (1) The candidate says he cannot know what he thinks because he does not yet know how the public thinks. This means that some candidates base their opinions on those of the voting public.

2. (1) The quote at the end of the passage declaring lame duck President Ronald Reagan to be irrelevant best supports the definition of a position holding little command or prestige.

Application

3. (4) Kennedy was killed before he attained lame duck status. All the others listed went through a period in their presidency when all knew that soon they would no longer be in that office.

4. (4) The power of eminent domain does not allow the government to take property away for any purpose other than for public use.

Analysis

5. (3) The critics described argue that the regulations take something from landowners. Eminent domain requires the government to pay for what it has taken.

Evaluation

6. (4) In applying eminent domain, government officials are allowing the public good to take precedence over the rights of the individual.

Application

7. (3) President Bush (who was part of the executive branch of government) prevented the judicial branch (the courts) from convicting the Iran Contra defendants. Choices (2), (4), and (5) each involved only one branch of the U.S. government. In choice (1), no government action was blocked.

8. (5) The Eighth Amendment's prohibition of "cruel and unusual punishment" is often invoked by people who oppose the death penalty.

9. (2) The Second Amendment prohibits only the federal government from banning the sale or ownership of weapons, a loophole that some local governments feel permits them to outlaw the possession of guns in their communities.

10. (4) The Sixth Amendment guarantees that those accused of a crime have a right to hear and see the witnesses against them. If the witness does not appear, the case may be thrown out.

Evaluation

11. (4) Choices (1), (2), (3), and (5) are either beliefs or facts concerning the availability of handguns. Only choice (4) represents a legal argument that concerns the constitutionality of owning a handgun.

Application

12. (3) The Ku Klux Klan engages in illegal, covert activity and does not seek to directly influence legislation as do the IBEW, ACLU, ILGWU, and political action committees.

Analysis

13. (5) The passage describes government officials as being guilty of fiscal irresponsibility, an opinion. Choices (1) and (2) are facts stated in the passage. Choices (3) and (4) are not expressed.

14. (5) The writer states that the framers of the U.S. Constitution did not anticipate the fiscal mismanagement of today's government. This suggests that an amendment to the Constitution might remedy the problem.

Evaluation

15. (5) Choice (5), that a balanced budget amendment might prevent the government from obtaining needed money during national emergencies, is the best. This argument has been expressed by opponents of such an amendment. Choices (1) and (2) are not the best arguments because neither the costliness nor the time needed should prevent a worthy amendment from passing. Choice (3) is not acceptable because the Constitution allows for amendments to be made. Choice (4) represents the opposite side of the argument.

Comprehension

16. (1) The passage says that certain freedoms were granted to Vietnam citizens only recently; therefore, citizens would not take them for granted.

Evaluation

17. (3) Although freedom is still restricted in Vietnam, the passage states that *doi moi* granted some new freedoms.

Application

18. (2) A precedent is an earlier legal action (in this situation a criminal case in Florida) that serves as a justification for a later action (the criminal case in Lake County).

Evaluation

19. (3) The passage indicates that the "victim" was a teenager, and possibly a minor, but not that the "defendant" was a minor.

Comprehension

20. (2) Citizens are most unhappy with the spending of state bodies, such as legislatures; therefore, they would most want to restrict it.

Analysis

21. (5) If people can see the results of a program, they are happier with it. (1) and (4) don't involve government spending; (2) and (3) are *problems* with local spending.

Application

22. (4) Conservatives do not like change, as demonstrated in the case of the farmers and small-town residents who were comfortable with the status quo.

23. (1) Radicals desire change, desire it immediately, and will go to extremes to get it. The students in the situation described staged rallies and marches to get the changes they wanted.

24. (2) Social improvement through welfare programs, national medical policies, and agricultural reforms describes the political orientation of a liberal.

Comprehension

25. (2) Control of the colony is changing because the British lease is up. Therefore, Great Britain must have had control through their lease from China.

Evaluation

26. (3) Communist China has an ongoing history of human rights violations, and the Chinese refugees living in Hong Kong would be well aware of it.

Analysis

27. (2) By agreement, Britain will withdraw and China won't take immediate control. The threat now is from loss of human resources as people flee.

Comprehension

28. (2) The passage mentions that the Twelfth Amendment was passed because of the rise of the political party system. Before the formal party system was established, the president and vice president could have had opposing political viewpoints. None of the other choices are supported by the information in the passage.

Analysis

29. (4) To ensure that a president has a vice president that is compatible, the presidential nominee is allowed to hand-pick a running mate.

Evaluation

30. (3) Sixty-six percent of the people responded that the federal government wastes the most tax dollars.

Comprehension

31. (3) According to the quote, death and taxes are constants and will always be with us. Choice (1) is an opinion. Choices (2) and (5) are true but are not the central meaning of the quote. Choice (4) shows no relationship between death and taxes as stated by the quote.

Analysis

32. (5) Of all the choices, only choice (5), that larger families pay more sales tax than smaller families, is a fact that does not contribute to the popularity of the tax. In fact, this is a frequent criticism of the tax.

33. (2) Only choice (2), which involves a luxury tax, increases the tax burden on the wealthy.

Evaluation

34. (3) Food is one of the basics that people need to live. The poor spend a greater proportion of their income for food than other classes. Therefore, to tax the poor for food is more unfair than taxing them for clothing, cigarettes, or public utility services. Since the poor generally cannot afford to purchase property, shelter is not a plausible choice.

Comprehension

35. (3) The passage describes and defines the origin of the term "estate." It also explains the purpose of the estate in government.

Application

36. (2) The passage defines the Fourth Estate as the public press. Today, the news media (of which ABC is a part) would be considered part of the press.

Analysis

37. (2) The nobility was considered to be an important part of the Estates General in France. The U.S. Constitution does not permit titles of nobility to be granted; therefore, the advisory body could not have been adopted in our government.

Evaluation

38. (2) As it is described, the Estates General was created to advise a king. The United States is a democracy, not a monarchy.

Comprehension

39. (2) The native Oregonian has moved to Florida and is no longer a resident of Oregon; therefore, he or she cannot run for the senate from Oregon.

Analysis

40. (5) The passage states that "Japan will never again wage war against other countries, or even maintain an army, navy, or air force." From this we can infer that Japan does not pay to support armed forces.

Application

41. (1) A dictator is a powerful chief executive. If Germany and Italy feared the return of dictatorships, their governments would have limited the executive branch.

Analysis

42. (3) The entire passage describes the influence of the U.S. Constitution around the world. None of the other opinions could be supported by the information provided.

43. (2) Shutting down the production of periodicals (magazines) contradicts the ideal of freedom of the press. Choices (1) and (3) allow *more* freedoms; choices (4) and (5) do not involve ideals cited in the passage.

Comprehension

44. (1) According to the key, the only state listed among the choices that has voted for a convention and then rescinded is Louisiana.

Evaluation

45. (1) The map points out that 34 (out of 50) states need to vote for the convention in order for it to be called. This represents a two-thirds majority. All the other choices except choice (3) are true statements but are not supported by information given on the map.

Analysis

46. (2) Had the amendment process been made too easy, the U.S. Constitution would have been burdened by numerous changes. The fact that only twenty-six out of more than 10,000 proposed amendments have been approved suggests that the framers believed only important and fundamental changes should be allowed.

BEHAVIORAL SCIENCES
Analysis

1. (4) Because there are no women past age thirty-five in firefighting, you can infer that, in the past, women did not actively pursue fire-fighting jobs. Choices (1), (2), (3), and (5) are not supported by the facts in the excerpt.

Comprehension

2. (1) A role model serves as an example or inspiration for others to follow.

3. (2) The girls are portrayed wearing braids and ponytails. This fact indicates that they are at the junior high school level.

Evaluation

4. (3) One of the observers at the door remarks that the children have a longer attention span because the teacher uses an artificial TV screen.

5. (1) The last sentence of the passage refers to cultural features—art, politics, manners, religion, and industry—as being affected by the Pacific. This suggests that the development of a culture is influenced by the natural environment in which it grows.

Analysis

6. (5) The passage tells us that Pacific islanders have little desire to master other men, one of the primary causes of wars.

Application

7. (3) Native Americans are the only group listed that demonstrates the same respect, awe, and fear toward nature that Pacific islanders do.

Evaluation

8. (1) According to Peter, happiness is determined by how much of our lives is spent in the state of *want to*. Of all the choices, only a walk in the park can be described as a *want to* activity.

Application

9. (4) In the passage, happiness is determined by how much of our lives is spent in the state of *want to*. People who are daring and who do many exciting things do them because they want to. Therefore, Peter would likely agree with choice (4).

Comprehension

10. (4) In this survey 37 more people claimed no religion in 1993 than in 1985—a 2% rise. No other category grew this much in number or percentage.

11. (2) Fifty-seven fewer Catholics were contacted in 1993 than in 1985—almost a 5% drop. No other category declined in number or percentage.

Evaluation

12. (5) Nontraditional religions would be included in the category "Other," which rose during the years shown. The table contradicts statements (1) and (4). The data shows nothing about membership in particular denominations or about church attendance.

Application

13. (5) Only choice (5), in which Vietnamese refugees learn to eat with forks, demonstrates a people acquiring the dominant culture of an area other than that of their birth and upbringing. Choices (1) and (2) are not instances of acquiring the dominant culture of an area other than that of one's birth. Choices (3) and (4) represent the opposite of acculturation.

14. (4) The Duke of Windsor is a title of nobility that can be attained only by birth. All of the other choices are examples of achieved status.

15. (3) Winning the title "most valuable player" is an honor that an athlete earns through individual effort.

Analysis

16. (2) The statement that neurotic and psychotic individuals have not learned to use defense mechanisms implies that these mechanisms serve a useful function by reducing conflicts and frustrations.

17. **(2)** Volunteers who help victims of disasters are members of a group that works together for a common purpose but does not share close personal relationships. This is the definition of a secondary group.

18. **(5)** The extended family consists of members other than the traditional mother, father, and children.

19. **(3)** The Lutheran Church is an institution organized to meet the religious needs of its members.

20. **(1)** A primary group can consist of any people who share highly personal relationships.

Analysis

21. **(3)** The only reasonable choice of those listed is the revoking of the ban forbidding mothers to have more than one child.

Comprehension

22. **(3)** The term "little emperors" implies that the children are treated royally. Such special treatment suggests that they are spoiled and self-centered.

Evaluation

23. **(2)** The need shown as "belongingness" precedes "esteem" on the hierarchy. This means that before people can experience admiration, they must feel that they are part of a group.

Application

24. **(1)** Appreciating one's place in history is another way of saying that one needs to realize and fulfill one's unique potential.

Comprehension

25. **(4)** When the authors refer to the difficulty of finding pediatricians, arranging repair appointments, and making child care arrangements, they are suggesting that society has not made adjustments to provide for the increase in the number of working mothers.

Analysis

26. **(5)** The statement that "the bottom line of the message remains clear to anyone who has lived through it—the normal mother, the caring mother, the *good* mother, is at home," suggests that because they hold jobs, working mothers are not normal, caring, or as good as mothers who stay home to raise their children.

Comprehension

27. **(5)** On the graph, the matrilineal line drops to zero at the level of plow agriculture. This suggests that families who trace their lineage through the females are not supported by farming.

28. **(4)** On the graph, the bilateral line is at its highest for the hunting and gathering category.

29. **(3)** The two lines (bilateral and patrilineal) meet at the level of horticulture. This fact shows that horticulture as a food-getting method is relied upon equally in both societies.

Evaluation

30. **(5)** The frequency of patrilineal-based societies is higher at the pastoralism and plow agriculture categories than are bilateral- and matrilineal-based societies.

Comprehension

31. **(5)** In the case shown, Martha states that her husband is a good provider. Therefore, economic pressures would not apply to Martha and her husband's situation.

Analysis

32. **(5)** The fact that the wealthy abuse their wives does not support the theory that economic pressure is one of the causes that leads a husband to abuse his wife.

33. **(4)** A researcher who concludes that improving schools will decrease social deviation is assuming that other factors, such as problems at home, are not the root causes of poor school performance and social deviation.

Application

34. **(4)** The only situation listed that demonstrates cultural diffusion is the spread of American rock music to all parts of the globe. Choices (1) and (2) show behavior that is the opposite of cultural diffusion. Choice (3) shows people willingly giving up their own culture within a new culture. Choice (5) does not illustrate the spreading of cultural elements.

35. **(3)** By spanking a child, a parent is teaching the child that a particular behavior is to be avoided, a characteristic of avoidance conditioning.

36. (1) The supervisor is praising a partially correct act in the hopes of gradually training the employee to perform the action correctly the first time. This demonstrates shaping.

Analysis

37. (4) According to the information in the chart, Chinese and Asian Indians have a far lower proportion of members with type O blood than do Native Americans. Also, Native Americans have no members with type B blood while Chinese and Asian Indians do. Together, these two facts appear to discredit the theory that Native Americans migrated to North America from Asia.

38. (4) Through natural selection, species that are best adapted to their living conditions survive, and those that don't adapt perish. This suggests that type O blood may have had benefits that enabled some Native Americans to survive, while those with other blood types did not.

Application

39. (2) Al's choosing to forget his unhappy childhood is a form of repression—keeping unpleasant thoughts that cause anxiety hidden in one's subconscious.

40. (5) Marie is acting in a way that is the opposite of the way she feels. This behavior demonstrates the use of the mechanism described as reaction formation.

41. (1) Jack is disguising the real reason for his failure to complete his homework assignment. This behavior demonstrates the use of rationalization.

42. (3) Victims of paranoia are said to have a personality disorder. By attributing their problem to other people, paranoiacs demonstrate projection in its extreme form. Displacement is the wrong choice because in displacement people transfer their frustrations—not blame—to other people or objects.

Analysis

43. (2) A psychologist who hypothesizes that her depressed clients might be helped by adopting pets is following step 2 of the scientific method—developing a theory.

44. (5) When psychologists decide that an experiment has proven a certain point they are drawing a conclusion—step 5 of the scientific method.

Comprehension

45. (2) According to the passage, neatness (orderliness) and a successful business (achievement) are characteristics related to environmental influences.

Analysis

46. (4) Two people who began life with the same biological makeup and who later find themselves in different environments are ideal subjects because a researcher can investigate whether or not the differences in their lives were caused by genes (nature) or by the environment (nurture).

47. (3) Because the twins were sentenced to an insane asylum rather than a prison, it can be inferred that their mental instability was a factor in their criminal activity.

GEOGRAPHY
Evaluation

1. (4) Cropland is the same as cultivated land. When compared to the region of the United States east of the Rocky Mountains, the West has relatively little tillable land.

Comprehension

2. (1) According to the map, tundra land is shown only in the far north areas.

Analysis

3. (1) According to the map, a great percentage of the land in northern Canada is forested. Forests are sources of lumber.

Evaluation

4. (5) Nuclear power plants are considered by many people to be human-made hazards. According to the criteria offered, "best towns" would not be located near human-made or natural hazards.

5. (4) Prohibiting the burning of leaves would help protect the environmental health of the area, the fourth criterion that a "best town" must meet.

6. (5) A tornado constitutes a natural hazard. Therefore, towns located near a tornado zone would not be desirable places in which to live.

7. (3) An *objective criterion* is one that is scientifically measurable and one in which a person's tastes, beliefs, or opinions are not involved. A *subjective criterion* depends on one's personal tastes, beliefs, or opinions. Of the choices given, "moderate local taxes" is the least objective because "moderate" can be interpreted different ways by different people.

Comprehension

8. (1) The lowest temperature for El Paso, Texas, is just below the 40 degree mark; the highest is at the 90 degree mark. This represents a difference of more than 50 degrees.

9. (4) The highest temperatures occur between 2:00 and 4:00 P.M.; this corresponds to midafternoon.

Evaluation

10. (3) El Paso, Texas, which has a continental climate, fluctuates more in temperature than does North Head, Washington, which has a marine climate.

Analysis

11. (5) The information describes a bell-shaped curve as representing a normal distribution. El Paso's temperature distribution conforms to a bell-shaped curve but North Head's does not. Therefore, North Head's temperature distribution is not considered to be representative of that of most U.S. cities (statement A). Also, if El Paso's average temperatures in January and July are considered to be normal, they are more likely to be representative of other U.S. cities than North Head's are (statement C).

Application

12. (4) North Head has a marine climate, one in which little variation in temperature occurs. San Francisco, also located near the ocean, is in the latitude nearest North Head, Washington; therefore, San Francisco would have a climate most like North Head's.

13. (2) Hawaii is described as having little noticeable difference in seasons and as being pleasantly warm. It is described neither as being cold nor hot; therefore, it would fall in the North Temperate Zone.

14. (3) Monsoons are described as heavy rains with intense heat, both features of the Torrid Zone.

15. (1) Alaska is located in the Northern Hemisphere. The regions in which only lichens might grow are the Antarctic Zone and the Arctic Zone. The Arctic Zone is in the Northern Hemisphere, as is Alaska. Choice (1) is therefore correct.

Comprehension

16. (5) According to the map's key, the darkest areas are the most humid. The largest dark area is located near the Equator (0 degrees latitude).

17. (2) A greater number of dark areas (areas of high humidity) can be found along the east coast than along the west coast. Therefore, the west coast can be described as more arid.

18. (4) The export share of newly industrialized nations jumped over 5 percentage points. No other area represented showed a percentage change as great.

Analysis

19. (3) Only low wages would account for industrialized countries becoming low-cost producers of raw steel and television sets. The conditions described in (1) and (2) are not shared by all NICs. Choices (4) and (5) are unrelated to the NICs growing importance in the world export market.

Comprehension

20. (3) The only individual country shown that lost a percentage of the world export market is the United States. Canada and Japan increased their shares. South Korea and Germany are not shown individually, so we can't be sure how their shares changed.

Analysis

21. (2) The only areas shown with larger shares of the 1990 market are Western Europe and other. Those categories each include many different countries, so it is unlikely that one nation within them provided more than 11.4% of world exports.

Evaluation

22. (2) The manufacture of semiconductors, personal computers, and jet engines involves the development of all highly complex products. The fact that the United States leads all nations in the export of these products suggests that the United States excels in exporting complex products.

Comprehension

23. (1) According to the map's key, Alaska had a ratio of between 151 and 200 doctors per 100,000 people.

Analysis

24. (2) South Dakota is the only state listed that had fewer than 151 doctors per 100,000 people in 1990.

25. (1) Doctors tend to be located in regions where a great concentration of people with money to afford their services live. These characteristics would favor Washington, D.C., over Mississippi. None of the other choices alone would adequately explain why Washington would have more doctors per 100,000 than Mississippi.

26. (5) The total land area of a state has no relationship to the number of doctors per 100,000 people. In fact, many states with large land areas have fewer doctors per 100,000 people than states with smaller land areas.

27. (4) Four out of the six states with a ratio of 200–299 doctors per 100,000 people are located in the Northeast and are urban and industrial. These are New York, Massachusetts, Connecticut, and Maryland.

28. (2) More neighboring states with a ratio of 100–149 doctors per 100,000 people are located in the Southeast than in any of the other regions listed. These rural, agricultural states include Arkansas, Louisiana, Mississippi, Alabama, Georgia, South Carolina, and North Carolina.

29. (4) Climate does not contribute directly to the number of doctors per 100,000 people. Each of the other factors would contribute to the number of doctors.

30. (4) The only fact listed that is causally related to a surplus of doctors is that salaries for doctors will decline dramatically. Based on the principle of supply and demand, a surplus in a commodity or service drives the price down. While choices (1), (2), (3), and (5) are possible trends in the medical industry, they are not effects of a doctor surplus.

Comprehension

31. (3) According to the passage, frigid air is heavy and highly pressurized. It generally brings clear, calm, cool weather.

32. (3) According to the passage, warm air leaving low pressure belts generally brings stormy, cloudy, warm, weather.

Application

33. (5) Movements by an army would be shown on a map that depicts borders between countries, states, or territories—a political map.

34. (2) A population map describes the distribution of the population of an area. Minority representation refers to population distribution.

35. (4) The annual snowfall of a region relates to the weather and would be shown on a weather map.

36. (1) A topographical map would indicate features of the terrain, which would be useful to a person unfamiliar with the land. None of the other maps would be useful to a soldier in helping him find his way around unfamiliar territory.

Analysis

37. (2) A mile equals 5,280 feet. If the delta spreads toward the Gulf of Mexico at the rate of 330 feet a year, it would take 16 years for the delta to spread one mile.

38. (4) Throughout history, civilizations have settled near bodies of water. Also, level land allows for an even distribution of population in addition to favorable farming conditions. Together these three features would contribute to deltas being highly desirable population centers. The three features do not explain choices (1), (2), (3), and (5).

39. (1) In clock time, as one moves from east to west, time is gained; as one moves from west to east, time is lost. This means that it is later in the East than the West. Therefore, the New Year would occur first in the East, followed by the Central, Mountain, and Pacific areas.

40. (4) Denver, located in the Mountain Time Zone, is one hour behind Chicago, which is located in the Central Time Zone. Therefore, when it is 1:00 A.M. in Chicago, it would be midnight in Denver.

41. (5) Dallas is in the Central Time Zone, which is two hours ahead of the Pacific Time Zone within which Seattle falls. Therefore, if it is 7:00 P.M. in Dallas, it would be 5:00 P.M. in Seattle.

42. (4) That Indiana is the only state exempt from observing daylight saving time cannot be concluded from the information given. If the entire state were exempt then Northwest Indiana would be exempt also, which is not the case. Choices (1), (2), (3), and (5) are all facts that can be concluded from the information provided.

Analysis

43. (3) The passage states that two or three quarts of water a day is what humans need to survive and adds that fifty gallons is the amount that some people use. From this fact you can infer that using more than three quarts of water per day constitutes misuse.

44. (2) Choices (1), (3), (4), and (5) are stated directly in the passage. Choice (2) involves a paradox because it seems contrary to common sense. (One would not think that a shortage of water could exist if most of the Earth's surface—nearly 75 percent—is made up of water.)

45. (5) The north central part of the United States includes the Great Lakes region—the region of the world with the greatest supply of fresh water. Although the Pacific Northwest, the Northeast, and the Middle Atlantic regions are located near oceans, ocean water is not fit for human consumption because of the salt content. The Southwest has the shortest supply of water of all the options.

ECONOMICS
Application

1. (2) These countries are like the authoritarian socialist model because property is public, not private, and individual choice is subordinated to state goals.

2. (5) Mercantilism, among other features, emphasizes commercial dominance, a goal that can be achieved in part by imposing tariffs on imported goods.

3. (1) An economy characterized by little or no government intervention is a purely capitalist economy.

4. (4) Under the sharecropping system, members of the lower class work land owned by a higher class in exchange for shelter and a share of the profits. This system most resembles the manorial feudal system.

Analysis

5. (4) A cost of living adjustment (COLA) is the only means listed by which wages may be kept in line with prices. None of the other choices involve keeping prices and wages parallel.

6. (1) If high unemployment is an indicator of a recession or depression and high unemployment is an indicator of a high GNP, it follows that high unemployment would indicate a low GNP, since fewer products are manufactured during recessionary periods.

Comprehension

7. (3) Equilibrium is the point at which the supply of a product equals demand. On the graph, the two lines cross at $700.

8. (5) The point at which the supply of VCRs equals demand is at ten units; therefore, the ideal number to stock is ten. None of the other amounts results in an equilibrium.

Analysis

9. (2) Seven hundred dollars is the market price for a VCR. If the price dropped to $600, Vic's could sell 12 units—two more than the usual demand.

Evaluation

10. (2) The graph concerns how price affects supply and demand. The principle illustrated in the graph is that as prices decrease, demand increases.

Analysis

11. (2) To decrease the amount of money in circulation during inflationary periods, the Fed would increase the reserve requirement, which requires commercial banks to hold more money and lend less. With fewer dollars in their hands, consumers will be forced to spend less.

12. (5) In order to make a profit, banks must charge higher rates for commercial loans than they have to pay to borrow money from the Fed. Of the rates listed, only a rate of 12 percent is higher than the 10 percent a member bank would pay.

Comprehension

13. (1) All of the figures indicate a total debt of more than 100 percent. That means that individual debt exceeded personal income.

14. (4) According to the information in the chart, 55 percent of the people polled favored a decrease in Social Security benefits.

15. (2) According to the information in the chart, 77 percent of the people polled were against a gasoline tax as a means to cut the deficit.

Evaluation

16. (1) In questions involving an increase in taxes as a way to reduce the deficit, an overwhelming number of those polled were against higher taxes (63 percent and 77 percent).

Analysis

17. (4) The only choice that explains why the DAT recorders did not generate sales is the unavailability of prerecorded tapes needed to use DATs. If consumers cannot use an item, little or no market exists for it.

Application

18. (3) Only choice (3), the failure of Sony's beta-formatted VCR, can be compared to the poor success of the DAT. Despite a reputation for having a sharper picture, the beta-formatted VCR failed largely because of the unavailability of beta videotapes in a market dominated by VHS-formatted VCRs.

19. (3) Frictional unemployment is caused by dissatisfied workers who quit their jobs, as in Clinton's situation.

20. (2) Structural unemployment is unemployment caused by a rapid change in the character of the economy. The change from a manufacturing emphasis to a servicing emphasis fits this definition.

21. (5) Hard-core unemployment is defined as a situation in which unemployment has become ingrained because of prolonged joblessness.

Comprehension

22. (2) The excerpt begins by describing the scenario if the United States went bankrupt. Therefore, you can infer that the author is referring to the United States when he describes its economy as being the most powerful on the face of the Earth.

Analysis

23. (3) The passage states that in the event of a default by the United States, "The dollar would drop so low that even Zaire wouldn't buy it." This implies that Zaire can afford to buy U.S. dollars only when the dollar is low, not high. Therefore, you can infer that Zaire is a poverty-stricken nation. Not enough information is provided for you to conclude that Zaire is the poorest nation on Earth.

Application

24. (2) A corporation's failure to take advantage of computers to improve efficiency demonstrates a failure to fully use available resources.

25. (4) A community college's training and retraining members of the work force would strengthen the trainable work force.

26. (5) Consumers who put off purchases affect the increase in aggregate demand that is necessary for the economy to grow.

27. (5) A group that forms a business to help its members save money on groceries would be described as a cooperative.

28. (1) Only in a sole proprietorship does a single owner have all responsibilities for business debts.

29. (4) According to the definitions given, in a limited partnership the owners are responsible for business debts only in proportion to the amount they have invested in the business. In a corporation, the individual owners are not personally responsible for the business's debts.

Comprehension

30. (1) In depicting the U.S. Congress headed in the wrong direction on a one-way street, the cartoonist is suggesting that Congress's taxing policies and the growth of the economy are at odds and that economic growth will suffer.

Evaluation

31. (2) By showing the economy headed in the right direction on a one-way street, the cartoonist suggests that the direction of the economy is right and congressional tax policy is wrong.

Analysis

32. (4) The cartoon shows nothing about budget deficits or government spending. It does, however, show Congress in a "taxing cab," so, Congress must be taxing citizens. The most likely use of new taxes is payments for programs and debt.

Application

33. (4) This cartoon focuses on the damaging effects of taxes on the economy, so we know the cartoonist would see the new taxes as a drain on the economy. New taxes tend to discourage spending, and as spending falls, so do business profits and the taxes gathered on them.

Analysis

34. (3) According to the figures in the graph, prices continued to rise in spite of the controls.

35. (4) The 1983 prices rose 40% by 1992. If this trend continues, they will rise almost as much again by the year 2000.

Comprehension

36. (2) The CPI measures the price of goods and services. *Price* and *cost* mean the same thing.

Comprehension

37. (5) The Dow industrials rose somewhat between 1980 and 1985, but the rise was not as high as later gains. For several years they did not rise at all.

Analysis

38. (3) The financial expert suggests that the airline industry may be temporarily affected by plane crashes, but the industry has never collapsed after one. Similarly, the Dow fell only for one year after the 1987 stock market crash.

Comprehension

39. (2) According to the chart, the year 1933 had the lowest GNP, level of personal income, and consumer price index, and the highest unemployment rate.

Analysis

40. (2) According to the chart, in 1941 GNP and personal income were up and unemployment was down. The economy was healthier than it had been in previous years, so you can infer that America's involvement in the war led to a healthier economy.

41. (2) The only answer that reasonably explains the low unemployment rate achieved between 1941 and 1945 is that factories at peak production capacity for the war effort had to hire many workers. None of the other choices alone can fully explain the increase in employment.

Evaluation

42. (2) According to the facts in the chart, the CPI for the 1930s and 1940s was between $40 and $50, compared to $100 for 1967. This is roughly half of the CPI of 1967 ($100).

Comprehension

43. (4) Based on the information provided, bond owners cannot vote, whereas holders of common stock can.

Evaluation

44. (4) According to the information in the passage, bond owners' repayments are guaranteed; however, the payments to stockholders are made at the discretion of the corporation, depending on profits. Moreover, preferred stock is guranteed priority over common stock, so the order of payment would be bond owners, preferred stockholders, and common stockholders.

45. (2) If a state such as Delaware attracts more corporations than any other, the implication is that the corporate climate is better there for those who manage corporations than for individual private investors. Choice (1) is incorrect because taxes are not discussed in the passage about the chartering process. Choice (3) is incorrect because investors do not always reside in the state in which a corporation is headquartered. Choice (4) would not explain Delaware's desirability as a home for corporations, and choice (5) cannot be inferred from the information given.